The Young Reader's
Encyclopedia
of Jewish History

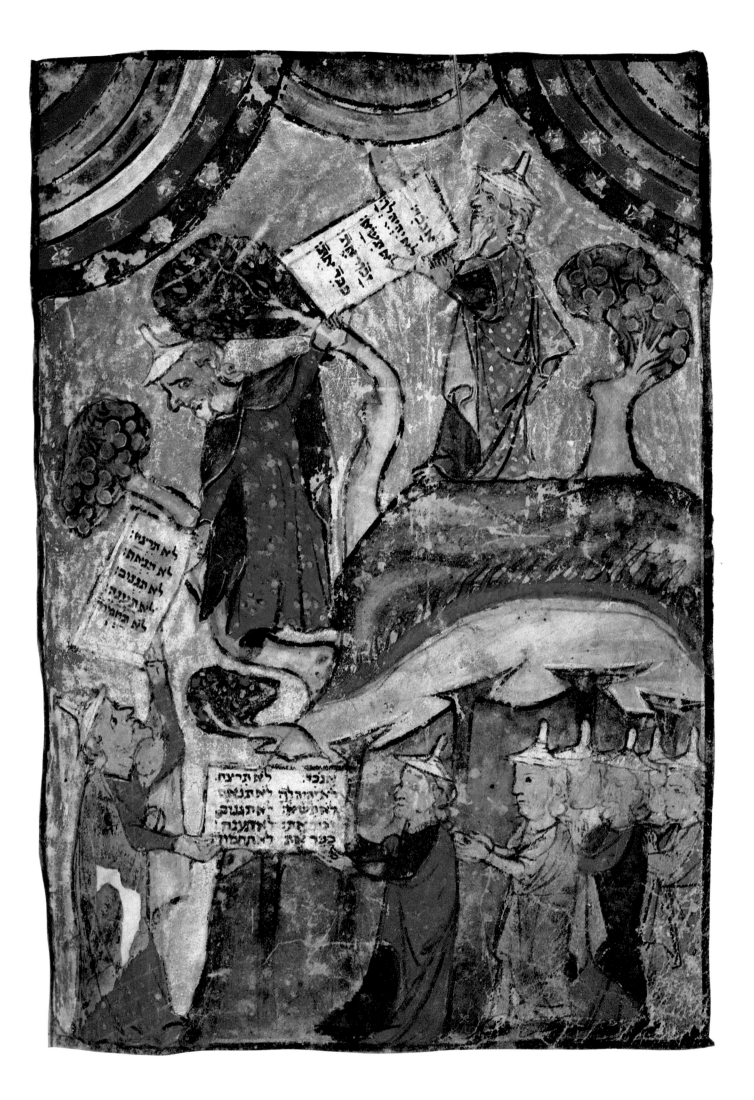

The Young Reader's Encyclopedia of Jewish History

Ilana Shamir, General Editor
Dr. Shlomo Shavit, Editor

Viking Kestrel

HOW TO USE *THE YOUNG READER'S ENCYCLOPEDIA OF JEWISH HISTORY*

The Young Reader's Encyclopedia of Jewish History tells the story of the Jewish people in Eretz Yisrael (the Land of Israel) and other countries from around 5000 B.C.E.—almost 7000 years ago—to the present. The initials B.C.E. (Before the Common Era) are used to mark the years before the birth of Jesus. They are counted backward from the time of the birth called the year 0 C.E. (Common Era). For example, when we say that something happened in the year 5000 B.C.E., we mean 5000 years before the birth of Jesus. If you add that number to the present year, you can see how long ago that was (for example, 1987 + 5000 = 6987 years ago).

The Encyclopedia can be read like a story from beginning to end, but chapters can also be read in any order. Each chapter contains terms which refer specifically to events or concepts in Jewish history and philosophy. These terms are generally explained in the text the first time they are used. An explanation also appears in the Glossary at the end of the book. Therefore, if you find a term that is not explained in context, look for it in the Glossary.

The language of the Jewish people is Hebrew, so Hebrew terms are used here. They appear in two forms: as they are pronounced in Hebrew (such as Eretz Yisrael), or in English translation if they are commonly used in English (such as the Land of Israel). The correct pronunciation of the Hebrew terms is given in the Glossary.

However, some Hebrew letters have no English equivalents. For example, "h," "ch," or "kh" may all stand for the same two Hebrew letters which are not exactly pronounced like any of these. These three different spellings are used because that is the way the words are traditionally spelled in English to approximate the guttural Hebrew sound. For the same reason, the Hebrew letter pronounced "tz" is sometimes represented by "z" alone.

The index at the end of the Encyclopedia tells you on which pages you can find information about the major periods, events, concepts, and personalities covered in this book.

VIKING KESTREL

Viking Penguin Inc., 40 West 23rd Street, New York, New York 10010, U.S.A.
Penguin Books Ltd, 27 Wrights Lane, London W8 5TZ (Publishing & Editorial) and
Harmondsworth, Middlesex, England (Distribution & Warehouse)
Penguin Books Australia Ltd, Ringwood, Victoria, Australia
Penguin Books Canada Limited, 2801 John Street, Markham, Ontario, Canada L3R 1B4
Penguin Books (N.Z.) Ltd, 182-190 Wairau Road, Auckland 10, New Zealand

First published in Israel by Massada Ltd. Publishers, 1987
First American edition published in 1987
Copyright © Massada Ltd. Publishers, 1987
All rights reserved

1 2 3 4 5 91 90 89 88 87

Library of Congress Cataloging-in-Publication Data
The young reader's encyclopedia of Jewish history.
Includes index.
Summary: An encyclopedia of information about main events, eras, and critical figures in Jewish history with 300 photographs, maps, charts, and drawings. Includes a glossary and chart of key events in Jewish history.
1. Jews—Dictionaries, Juvenile. [1. Jews—History—Dictionaries and encyclopedias] I. Shamir, Ilana. II. Shavit, Shlomo
DS102.8.Y68 1987   909'.04924'00321   87-10599
ISBN 0-670-81738-4

Printed in Israel by Peli Printing Works Ltd.

Title page picture: Moses on Mount Sinai, where the people of Israel undertook to follow God's commandments. Bible illumination from the Regensburg Manuscript, 14th century.

Picture Editor: Naama Cifroni
Translators: Sara Kitai, Avryl Kriss
Design: Doreet Scharfstein
Jacket Design: Yael Lior
Proofreader: Ruth Lidor

CONTENTS

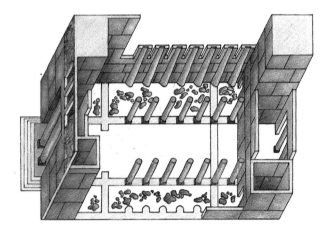

Introduction

The Jewish nation is both one of the oldest in the world and one of the youngest; it regained its independence in its ancient homeland less than forty years ago.

The Bible tells us of the early generations: the patriarchs and the Exodus from Egypt, the conquest and settlement of Eretz Yisrael, the Land of Israel. In the Land of Israel, the tribes became a nation and established a state, with Jerusalem as its capital and its Temple as the religious center for the entire nation. But the state was not to remain independent for long. One after the other, foreign nations conquered and ruled the land: the Assyrians, Babylonians, Persians, Greeks, and Romans. Yet the Jewish people remained in the Land of Israel where they developed a unique way of life based on belief in one God.

The tragedy of the nation began in the year 70 C.E., when the Romans burned the Temple and destroyed Jerusalem. After that time, fewer and fewer Jews lived in the Land of Israel, and the number became even smaller when the Christian Byzantine Emperor Constantine conquered the region; the number fell again when it was taken by the Arabs in 634 C.E. The Jews slowly became a minority in their own land.

The Jewish people, deprived of their homeland, wandered throughout the world to whatever countries would have them. But wherever they went, they preserved their national identity. Separated from the lost homeland, they established Jewish communities. All of them celebrated the Sabbath and the same holidays and recited the same Hebrew prayers. To the people around them they appeared alien—foreigners whose true homeland was somewhere else. They were considered infidels because they were unwilling to convert to Christianity or Islam. And even the Jews saw themselves as aliens, and prayed every day for God to bring them back to Eretz Yisrael, where they would reestablish an independent nation.

Great changes have taken place over the past two hundred years. Jews were recognized as equal citizens, first by the United States of America in 1783, then by France in 1791, and later by other Western countries. But at the same time, there were more and more attacks on the Jews—particularly in Eastern Europe, where most of the Jews in the world lived. And so, about one hundred years ago, large numbers of Jews began to leave Eastern Europe, most of them sailing for the United States.

A few decided to immigrate to Eretz Yisrael (which was then a poor and neglected country ruled by the Turks). These Jews had a vision: to renew Jewish settlement in the Land of Israel so that in time the nation could regain its independence in its ancient homeland. But most of the Jews from Eastern Europe moved westward, the majority of them settling in the United States. In just over thirty years, from 1884–1921, the Jewish community in America became the largest in the world.

In 1917, during World War I, the British conquered the Land of Israel, then known as Palestine, and promised to help the Jews establish a national homeland in the country. Three years later, the United States government put a quota on the number of immigrants that would be allowed into the country. Anti-Semitism was then greatly increasing in Europe, and reached new heights when the Nazis rose to power in Germany in 1933. More and more Jews decided to make their home in Eretz Yisrael. As the Jewish community there grew larger, the Arab opposition grew stronger, and the British began to limit the number of Jewish immigrants to Palestine. The Jews of Europe now had no place to go.

In 1939, World War II broke out, and the Nazis committed the greatest crime ever against the Jewish people. Their leaders planned to kill every Jew under their control. This mass murder—the Holocaust—was systematically carried out from 1942 until the very end of the war in 1945.

This unimaginable tragedy may have been one of the reasons that the United Nations General Assembly decided, at the end of 1947, to allow the Jews to establish an independent state in Eretz Yisrael. The Arabs would not accept this decision and they immediately attacked. Against overwhelming odds, the Jewish community managed to defend itself. In 1948 the State of Israel was established, aided by Jews all over the world, and particularly by those in the United States.

With the end of the War of Independence, it was time to build and grow. At the same time, homes and jobs had to be found for the hundreds of thousands of Jews from Europe and Muslim lands who wanted to settle in the new state. Since then, Israel has developed into a modern nation, whose Arab neighbors—except for Egypt—are still at war with it and refuse to recognize Israel's right to exist.

Although the return to Eretz Yisrael was a dream cherished by Jews throughout the ages, only about a third of the world's Jewish population now lives in Israel; nearly half live in the United States. Israel sees itself as the home of the Jewish people. Its Law of Return guarantees immediate citizenship to Jews from all over the world. The interdependence of the State of Israel and Jews the world over is a central theme underlying Jewish life today.

Shlomo Shavit
Jerusalem, 1987

1

FROM NOMADIC TRIBES TO A NATION

The prehistoric age in the Land of Israel, or *Eretz Yisrael* in Hebrew, lasted until about 7,000 years ago. During this time most of the people lived in small groups. They roamed from place to place and made their living from hunting and gathering food. Stone was the main material from which they made their tools. That is why this period is called the "Stone Age." Remains of people who lived then have been found in caves on Mount Carmel. Sites where they lived have also been found, as well as the tools they used, made of stones and animal bones, and beautiful necklaces made from teeth and shells.

Groups of nomads began to settle in permanent places toward the end of the Stone Age. They built houses and forts from stone. Their major innovation was the use of clay to produce vessels for storage and cooking. Utensils, fossilized seeds, animal bones, and sickle blades were found in their settlements. This shows us that in addition to hunting and herding, they also grew crops. Idols of the gods they believed in were also found in these sites.

After the Stone Age came the "Chalcolithic Period," which lasted up to 3300 B.C.E. People learned then to make tools from copper (*chalco* in Greek). They grazed their flocks in pastures around the settlements where they lived. Their houses were made from mud bricks and they decorated the walls with colorful paintings. Objects made from ivory were found in these houses, as well as certain tools which prove to us that they developed dairies and made cheese.

Tools, decorations, figures, and beautiful items of worship made by Chalcolithic artisans have also been found in a cave in the Judean desert, called the "Treasure Cave." The items may have belonged to the temple at nearby Ein Gedi. They were probably hidden in the cave for safekeeping. The Chalcolithic settlements eventually disappeared. We don't know why.

At the end of this period, the historic period began—when people started writing down history. It happened in Eretz Yisrael, then called Canaan, about 5,000 years ago. Walled towns with temples, houses, and workshops were built throughout the country. Unwalled settlements were built alongside them. The people grew grapes and olives, and cultivated grain and beans using plows and oxen. There were strong trading ties between the Kingdom of Egypt and Canaan. Pottery from Eretz Yisrael, thought to have held farm produce, has been found in graves in Egypt, and Egyptian pottery has also been

This clay figure of a seated woman was carved at the end of the Stone Age. The woman is wearing a cloak and has a mask over her face. She is thought to be a mother-goddess.

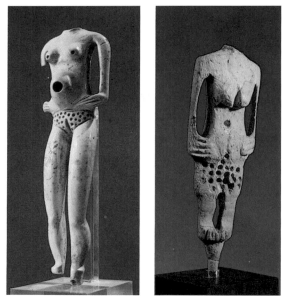

These ivory figures of worship were found on the banks of the Beersheba River. The people who lived here were experts at carving objects from ivory.

9

A collection of royal letters was discovered in Egypt. They tell us about the Egyptian rule in Canaan and the rivalry among the city-states. One of the letters is shown in the photograph above. The letters were written in cuneiform in the Akkadian language, which was the international language in those days.

The decorated mace-head on the far right was found in the "Treasure Cave."

Pottery pieces from Greece and Cyprus, found in Eretz Yisrael, are shown on the right. They were imported not only for their beauty, but also because they contained oils and perfumes.

discovered in Eretz Yisrael.

In the 24th century B.C.E., the cities were abandoned for some unknown reason, and the towns and farming culture died out. But about 200 years later, the country was again settled by groups of farmers, shepherds, and hunters. Later, cities and villages began to appear again along the Mediterranean coast and in the valleys, spreading inland. The country was divided into large city-states. These were surrounded by heavy walls with large entrance gates, leading to grand palaces, temples, and other buildings. Inside the buildings, items of worship, jewelry and pottery, bronze and ivory have been found. We can learn from these how wealthy the rulers of the city-states were, and how trade flourished, because many of the objects came from distant countries.

Later on, people called the Hyksos passed through Canaan and down the Nile, taking control over Canaan and Egypt. The Egyptians soon freed themselves from the Hyksos and then conquered Canaan. The

Egyptian Pharaohs, or kings, ruled Canaan for about 350 years (1550–1200 B.C.E.). Sometimes the people who lived in the Canaanite city-states rose up and revolted against the Pharaohs, but they were subdued by the Egyptian armies. The journey of Pharaoh Thutmose III to Megiddo in 1482 B.C.E. was especially important because that was when the first Egyptian administration was set up in Canaan.

Around 1200 B.C.E. the Egyptians left Canaan. Their place was soon filled by the Philistines and the Israelites.

The Patriarchs and the Exodus from Egypt

Who were the Patriarchs of the Jewish people? The Bible tells us that the Patriarchs—Abraham, Isaac, and Jacob—were herders of sheep, cattle, and camels. They lived in large families, or clans, on the edge of the Judean desert, wandering short distances with their flocks. They made their living from farm animals, crafts, and bartering. They left Eretz Yisrael for Egypt

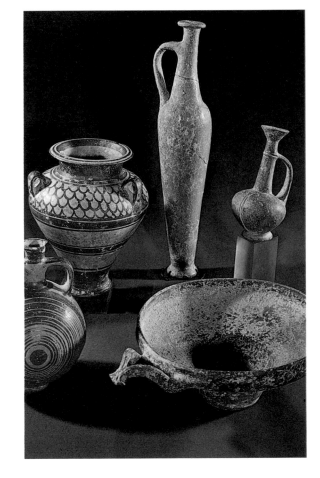

because of famine.

Some historians believe that the families of the sons of Jacob lived in Egypt when it was ruled by the Hyksos. The story of when the Israelites were slaves in Egypt, and their departure from Egypt (the Exodus), is not mentioned in Egyptian writings. However, work on the great city of Ramses, built by the Pharaoh Ramses II in the 13th century, may have been carried out by Israelite slaves.

Over the generations, legends of miraculous events have accompanied the story of the Exodus. This is why some historians argue that the Israelites did not all wander together in the desert as a single group. There

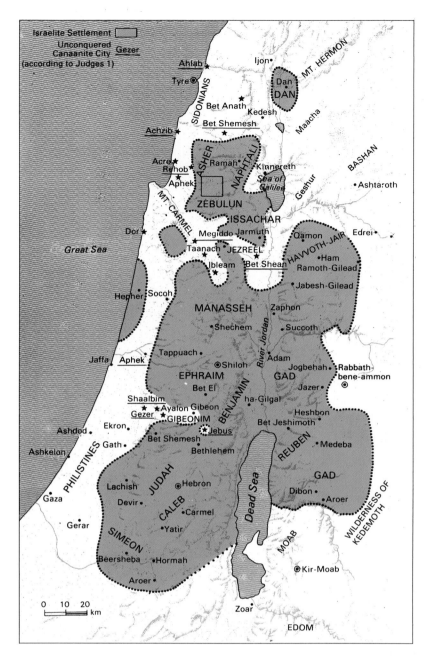

are also disagreements on the date of the Exodus. We are not even sure of the exact sites of two important places mentioned in the Bible—the Red Sea and Mount Sinai. The Bible does not say exactly where Mount Sinai is, but scholars believe it to be Mount Moses, in the Sinai Peninsula.

Despite these uncertainties, the Revelation at Sinai was a very important event in the history and the faith of the People of Israel. Here—according to the Bible—a holy pledge, or Covenant, was made between God and the Israelites. It was here that they were presented with the Torah (The Book of the Covenant) and became "the chosen people"—"chosen" by God to carry the burden of his commandments. Moses is described in the Bible as

the leader and "The First Among the Prophets." He led his people out of Egypt and taught them the belief in only one God, which is called monotheism.

THE ISRAELITES SETTLE IN CANAAN

The Israelites and the Philistines began to settle in Canaan at some point toward the end of the 13th century B.C.E., as the Egyptians left the area. The two nations started taking over more and more land, and it was not long before serious fighting broke out between them.

According to the Bible, all of Israel's twelve tribes together took part in the battle for the Land of Israel. However, some scholars believe that nomadic Israelite families started settling in the hilly

The area in which the Israelites settled is shown in the map above.

Tel el-Qudayrat, above left, is the largest oasis in the northern part of the Sinai Desert. This is thought to be Kadesh Barnea, where, according to the Bible, the Israelites camped on their way to the Promised Land.

Mount Moses, pictured at left, in the Sinai Peninsula.

11

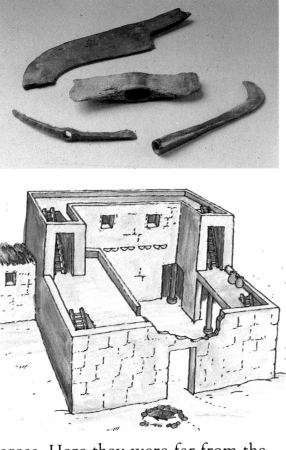

Only a few iron tools, like the knives and hatchets shown in this photograph, were found at sites of the Israelite settlements. During this time, bronze was the main metal they used.

This model shows a typical Israelite house of the Settlement period. There is an open courtyard where they kept their animals. On both sides of the courtyard, long rooms were built as shelters for the animals in bad weather. The people lived in the rooms at the back. They built a group of houses like this one in a circle for protection.

areas. Here they were far from the other peoples who lived in Canaan, including the Philistines. Eventually, these Israelite families formed tribes, each with its own territory. Some tribes were able to conquer several Canaanite city-states. But there were the Philistines, who lived along the southern coast in five city-states. The Philistines had a strong army and weapons made of iron, which was hardly known then to the Israelites. This gave the Philistines an advantage over the Israelites. At that time, the tribes of Israel were not united. Some tribes were harassed by neighboring nations.

The Judges were the leaders of the tribes through these difficult times. One of them was Deborah. It is said that when Judge Barak, son of Avinoam, agreed to go out and fight Cicera, commander of the army of the King of Canaan, it was on condition that she went with him.

The tribes of Israel eventually managed to unite under one leader in order to be strong enough to fight the Philistines. But at the end of the 11th century B.C.E., the Israelites were defeated, the Ark of the Covenant was captured, and their religious center at Shilo was destroyed. After this the Israelites demanded to be ruled by a king, like the other nations around them.

2

THE PEOPLE OF ISRAEL SET UP KINGDOMS

Saul was the first king to rule over all the tribes of Israel. Appointed king by Samuel the Prophet, he reigned from 1025 to 1004 B.C.E. It took him only a few years to organize his kingdom. To manage the wars against the Philistines, Saul built up an army. He made the place of his birth, Gibeah, the royal capital. Members of his tribe, Benjamin, helped him rule the kingdom. His army was finally defeated in a bloody battle, in which Saul himself and three of his sons were killed.

THE KINGDOM OF DAVID AND SOLOMON

David, Saul's son-in-law, was the next king of Israel. He was appointed king by the leaders of the tribes and reigned for 30 years. David joined all the tribes together under one strong government. He also built up a strong army, and managed to push the Philistines out of the Israelite territories. The land he conquered stretched eastward to Transjordan and northward to the Lebanon. David, and his son Solomon who reigned after him, controlled the main trading routes in Eretz Yisrael: the Via Maris (the "Coastal Road") and the "King's Highway," as well as Mediterranean and Red Sea ports. They set up trading links with neighboring rulers, including the Queen of Sheba in Africa. Ivory, gold, and rare plants and animals were brought from these places.

Jerusalem was captured by David from the Jebusites. It was chosen as the capital and center of government and culture, both because it was high up in the hills and therefore easy to defend, and because it was outside the territory of any of the tribes. David strengthened the city's protective walls and Solomon doubled its size and built many public buildings. By building the Temple in Jerusalem, Solomon gave great religious importance to the city for all the nation. The Tent of the Congregation and the Ark of the Covenant, which the Israelites had taken with them everywhere since

Megiddo was on the "Via Maris." Therefore it became a very important city, here reconstructed by an American expedition in the 1930s. The city was built on a hill and surrounded by walls. The buildings covered with roofs in the front are storerooms. At the back is the walled palace and next to it are the stables and paddocks.

This capital—the uppermost part of a column—is typical of Israelite buildings found in royal centers such as Megiddo, Hazor, Samaria, and Jerusalem, from the 10th century B.C.E.

The Kingdom, set up almost one hundred years before, was now split into two sister kingdoms—Yisrael and Yehudah, known in English as Israel and Judah.

THE KINGDOM OF ISRAEL

Jeroboam, son of Nebat, set up the Kingdom of Israel. During its first fifty years, the Kingdom of Israel

Division in the Kingdom caused changes in the map. The Kingdom of Judah is made up of the tribes of Judah and Benjamin. All the other tribes united to form the Kingdom of Israel.

A winged sphinx made of ivory, above right, from a large collection of ivory pieces found in Samaria. The Bible tells of the ivory objects used by the kings of Israel and Judah.

At right is a pillared building from King Ahab's time, discovered at Hazor. Apparently it was used as a royal storehouse.

their nomadic period in the desert, were placed in the Temple. A ceremony was held to make the house of worship a Holy Place.

The Kingdom of Solomon was divided into twelve districts. These divisions were not made according to the wishes of the tribes, but to allow the royal officials to collect taxes easily.

There were two main types of taxes: a tax on the property the people owned, and a labor tax which forced people to work on large building projects. These taxes were very hard for the people to bear. Eventually, some of the people began to rise up against their ruler. Revolts broke out in full force when Rehoboam, Solomon's son, came to the throne in 928 B.C.E. Rehoboam arrived in Shechem, where, "all Israel had come to make him King" (Kings I 12:1). The people said they would accept him as king on condition that he make their taxes easier. His advisors suggested that he agree with their demands for the time being.

Rehoboam refused. This made the people very angry and some of them

was constantly at war with the Kingdom of Judah. Only when Omri came to the throne in 882 B.C.E. did the kingdom know peaceful times. Omri made a pact with Judah, which was later made stronger when the son of the King of Judah married Omri's daughter, Athaliah. When there were no wars between Judah and Israel, Omri warred with neighboring countries and expanded his territory. He made treaties with the Phoenician kingdoms of Tyre and Sidon. His son, Ahab, married Jezebel, daughter of the King of Sidon. Omri built a new capital at Samaria and surrounded it with massive fortifications to protect himself and display his power. Ahab, who reigned from 871 to 852 B.C.E., continued his father's policies and building projects.

The Kingdom of Israel prospered and grew wealthy. This, together with the close ties with Phoenicia, led to changes in Jewish culture and in the customs of the upper classes. King Ahab became a tyrant. Queen Jezebel brought with her to Samaria idols of the gods that the people of Sidon worshipped—Baal, lord of the gods, and Ashtoreth, goddess of fertility. Temples to these gods were built and many priests and prophets worshipped in them. This went against the Israelite belief in one god.

Led by Elijah, the prophets of Israel fought the Baal priests and prophets, and caused their massacre on Mount Carmel. They in turn were persecuted and killed, and even

Elijah was forced to flee. Elisha, his successor, had much support from the people and decided to lead a revolt. He ordered Jehu, the minister of war, to murder Ahab's family in revenge for the blood of the prophets.

The Kingdom of Israel was weakened by frequent changes in the dynasty and by unrest among the people. The country was also attacked by the Arameans, who lived to the north. Only when the Assyrian Empire threatened both Israel and Judah (and also the Arameans) with war did they join forces. But Tiglath Pileser III, King of Assyria, defeated them all in 732 B.C.E. He exiled some of the Israelites to distant provinces and

allowed foreigners to settle in their stead. The Kingdom of Israel was limited to the Mount Ephraim area, and Hoshea, son of Elah, was made king. He refused to accept Assyrian rule and stopped paying taxes. This made the Assyrians attack and destroy his kingdom in 720 B.C.E., and the remaining Israelites were exiled.

THE KINGDOM OF JUDAH

The Kingdom of Judah was neither as large nor as wealthy as the Kingdom of Israel, but its monarchy was continually in the hands of the House of David. The kingdom began to prosper during the reign of King Asa, Rehoboam's grandson, who ruled from 908 to 867 B.C.E. There were trading links with Tyre and the city-states of Philistia. As in the

Kingdom of Israel, people of Judah began to worship pagan gods. There were struggles between the priests and the king, and in the end all idol-worship was removed from Jerusalem.

Jehoshaphat, son of Asa, signed a peace treaty with Omri and Ahab, kings of Israel. He strengthened his army and improved fortifications. Like his father he tried to stop idol-worship. He also created a supreme court in Jerusalem, which gave the city great importance.

Above are stone weights of different values, which were discovered at sites throughout Judah. Simple scales and stones such as these were used to weigh jewelry and coins.

Center: Exiles on their way to Assyria are shown in this Assyrian engraving.

Many sets of household pottery, like the ones shown in the photograph at far left, were found in houses throughout the Kingdom of Judah.

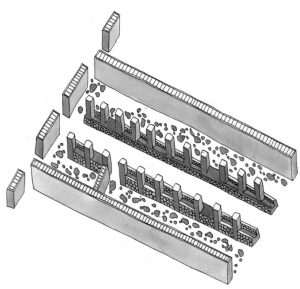

The Assyrian conquest of Lachish in 701 B.C.E. is described in a stone relief (shown at far right), which was discovered inside the palace of Sennacherib, King of Assyria. At right is a copy of the relief. It shows the defenders on the tower shooting arrows at their attackers, who are bringing up a battering ram to the walls of the city.

Storehouses were discovered in Beersheba, a city in the Kingdom of Judah. On the right is a drawing of one of them. The center hall was apparently a corridor for donkey caravans.

The inscription on the far right describes the last moments of work as the Siloam tunnel in Jerusalem was being dug. The tunnel (500 meters long) was designed to take the waters of the Gihon fountain into the city. The winding tunnel was dug at the time of King Hezekiah, and it still works today.

Under the reign of Uzziah, who ruled from 769 to 733 B.C.E., Judah became even more stable. He controlled the trading routes along the coast and through the southern region of the country (the Negev) and encouraged people to set up farms in different parts of the country.

In those days, the prophets had great influence on the kings. They always said what they thought, even when they were unpopular. They did not attack the idea of the monarchy itself. However, they would not accept cruel deeds by the kings, and they favored moral and religious changes. The most important of these changes took place during the reigns of Hezekiah and Josiah. King Hezekiah cut down idol-worship, which had been forced on Judah by the Assyrians. He tried

to rebel against Assyria, and even though he managed to fortify Jerusalem, he was defeated in 701 B.C.E. by the Assyrian army, although Jerusalem itself was not conquered.

About one hundred years later, at a time when Assyria was weak, the king of Judah, Josiah, conquered Ephraim and Sameria from the Assyrians, and made them part of Judah. He repaired the Holy Temple in an effort to keep alive the religion and nationhood of the people.

After King Josiah's death, a disagreement broke out between those people who favored Egypt and those who supported Babylonia— they were both at war with each other. They fought about the territories which once belonged to the Assyrian Empire. However, the Babylonian King Nebuchadnezzar besieged Jerusalem in 598 B.C.E. and exiled King Jehoiachin. Three years later, Judah rebelled against Babylonia, hoping for help from Egypt. Nebuchadnezzar invaded the country, and in 586 B.C.E. he burned the Temple and exiled most of the Jewish people. The Kingdom of Judah was destroyed.

3

FROM THE BABYLONIAN EXILE THROUGH THE RETURN TO ZION

The Babylonians turned Jerusalem into a heap of ruins (586 B.C.E.). Judah became a district of the Babylonian Kingdom. Gedaliah, son of Ahikam, a member of a noble Judean family, was appointed commissioner by the Babylonians. He was murdered by conspirators because he was considered to be a representative of the Babylonians. The murder created great fear and apprehension, and what remained of the Judean population fled to Egypt, fearful of Babylonian revenge.

EXILE IN BABYLON

Like the Assyrians before them, the Babylonians exiled peoples from their conquered lands. They did this in order to prevent the conquered peoples from organizing themselves once more against Babylon, and to break their links with their homeland. Despite this, even in Babylonia, the exiles from Judah remained united. Most of them were settled near the Hebar River—a large canal near the city of Nippur, between Assyria and Babylonia. Most of them were farmers and traders.

During their long exile, the captives got used to their new surroundings. However, they felt bitter and humiliated by their captivity and by the destruction of the Temple. They believed that they were being punished for the sins of their fathers, and that in order to be worthy of returning once more to their own land, they would have to mend their ways.

The exiles built up their hopes as a people and as a religion, and were

strengthened by goals such as the renewal of the Kingdom of David and the rebuilding of the Temple. The prophets, who were exiled with the people, gave them some hope with their prophecies. Jehoiachin, a descendant of the House of David, who was once the king of Judah, remained the leader of the people, even in captivity.

The prophet Jeremiah lamenting the destruction of the Temple. This painting is by the Dutch painter Rembrandt (1606–1669).

Cyrus' policy toward the peoples living in his kingdom is written on this clay cylinder. It was discovered in 1890.

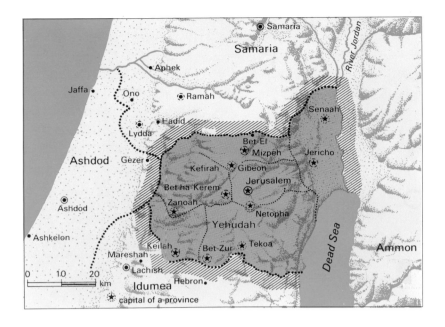

THE RETURN TO ZION

In 539 B.C.E., Cyrus, King of Persia, conquered Babylonia. His policy toward the peoples living in the areas he conquered was to allow them to live according to their own tradition. This policy, also mentioned in the Bible, in the book of Nehemiah, led to high hopes among the exiles. Cyrus indeed declared that the Jews of Babylonia were free to return to Jerusalem and to rebuild their Temple. Many Jews, led by Sheshbazzar, of the House of David, left Babylonia for Judah.

During this period the Land of Israel was part of the Persian satrapy (or territory) of Abar-nahara, which means "across the river." It stretched from the river Euphrates to Egypt. Judah covered only a small part of it.

About half a year after their arrival, a festive ceremony was held in Jerusalem to mark the beginning of the rebuilding of the Temple. However, work on the Temple was soon stopped. The people who lived on Mount Ephraim (later known as Samaritans) also wanted to take part, claiming that they, too, worshipped the God of Israel. Those who had returned from captivity refused to agree to this, arguing that only they had been permitted to rebuild the Temple. Yet it seems that the real reason was that they

suspected the Samaritans of worshipping other gods. Through threats and harassment, the Samaritans managed to halt the construction of the Temple. Only when Darius I became king of Persia in 522 B.C.E. did the Jews begin once more the work of rebuilding the Temple. In the month of Adar (March–April) of 516 B.C.E., the second Temple was completed. This became a symbol of the hope that the Kingdom of David would be renewed.

During the next sixty years, the Jews began to have closer dealings with the local population, whom they had rejected at first, and some Jews even adopted their culture.

In the year 458 B.C.E., a group of several thousand returning Jews, led by Ezra, arrived in Jerusalem.

It seems that the King of Persia, Artaxerxes, encouraged more Jews to return to Eretz Yisrael, after serious revolts had broken out against him in Egypt. By doing this he hoped to win the support of the inhabitants of Judah, which was close to Egypt.

Ezra was worried about the Jews mixing with the local population and decided to fight against it. Therefore he gathered all the people together at a meeting in which they read and explained the Torah—the written law which was, according to Jewish belief, given to Moses at the

Revelation on Mount Sinai.

A few years later, Nehemiah, who had been cupbearer of the King of Persia, was appointed governor of Judah. He was given permission to rebuild Jerusalem. The first thing he did was to repair the destroyed city walls. The task was carried out by groups of volunteers, and was completed in only 52 days. Next, he forced one out of every ten inhabitants of the towns of Judah to move to Jerusalem. Nehemiah also divided farmland among the people. This made him very popular with the ordinary people. Now Nehemiah could begin to put Temple worship in order and continue the work which Ezra had begun. He made a covenant with the people which included a pledge that Jews would remain separate from the others, that they would observe the Sabbath, and that they would worship properly at the Temple.

THE CONQUEST OF ALEXANDER

Alexander the Great, King of Macedonia, set out from the west to

fight against the Persians in the east. He intended to conquer all the territory ruled by the Persians. In 333 B.C.E. he defeated the Persians at the Battle of Issus, which is today in the north of Syria. This opened the way for him to Syria, Eretz Yisrael, and Egypt. Several Jewish writings mention the fate of the Jews of the Land of Israel after Alexander's conquest. They all tell of the greatness of the God of Israel, to whom even Alexander, the famous conqueror, paid respect. Since Alexander allowed the peoples he conquered to run their own affairs,

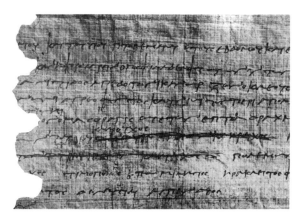

it is probable that he gave the Jews the same freedom which they had enjoyed under Persian rule.

Alexander died in 323 B.C.E. His senior generals, the *Diadochi* (Greek for "successors"), began a struggle

When the Persians ruled the country, beautiful pottery, like the piece in the picture far left, was brought from Athens and sold in the coastal cities of Eretz Yisrael.

Below is the end of a gold Persian earring, found in Ashdod, on the coast. The jewelry was either brought by Persian soldiers or by people serving in the local government, or was made by local jewelers who copied the Persian style.

The silver coin, above center, bears the name of Alexander the Great. On one side is the Greek god Zeus, seated on his throne. To his right is a Greek inscription, "Coin of Alexander." Beneath the eagle there is the Phoenician inscription "Acre 34," giving the city and the year in which the coin was minted (probably 312 B.C.E.). Alexander appears on the other side of the coin.

Center: Alexander the Great is shown on a mosaic discovered at Pompeii—a city in Italy which was destroyed by a volcano in the first century B.C.E.

The bill of sale for a maidservant, on the left—a papyrus from the archives of Zeno.

19

This Hellenistic-style clay figure of Aphrodite, the Greek goddess of love and fertility, probably from the end of the 4th century B.C.E., was found on Mount Carmel. It shows how widespread the worship of Aphrodite was.

The lioness, above right, is a relief from Qasr al'Abd (Fortress of the Servant), apparently built by Hyrcanus, son of Tobiah, at the beginning of the 2nd century B.C.E.

for the crown. This was a time of great unrest in the Land of Israel.

Situated between Egypt and Syria, the Land was in the path of Alexander's warring successors—the Seleucids from Syria and the Ptolemies from Egypt. In the next twenty years, the Land underwent five changes of ruler. It then passed into the hands of the Ptolemies. The Ptolemies ruled the Land of Israel for most of the 3rd century B.C.E. We can learn about the way they ran their empire from reports written on papiri by Zeno, a high Egyptian official, whose archives were discovered at Faiyum, Egypt. The country was divided into small districts, where Jews and Samaritans lived and were allowed some freedom by the Ptolemies, who were concerned with two main problems:

receiving their taxes regularly, and fighting off the constant threat from the Seleucids. The first problem was solved by using tax collectors. These were members of rich and important families who promised to give a certain amount of money to the treasury. They then tried to collect as many taxes as possible and kept the difference between what they collected and what they had promised to the treasury. One of these wealthy families was the Jewish family of Tobiah. Remains of their palace, decorated in the Hellenistic style with sculptures and animal reliefs, were found in Jordan.

In order to control the Land of Israel and to prevent the Seleucids from conquering it, the Ptolemies kept an army of mercenaries (paid soldiers) in the country's fortresses and main cities. There were also military colonies, some of which had been founded during the time of Alexander. In exchange for agreeing to serve in the army whenever asked, those who settled in these colonies received land from the king, and were in charge of the day-to-day security of their region.

The Hellenistic culture (the word *Hellas* means Greece in the Greek language) spread through the country. The Jews, like the other peoples in the area, were unable to keep out these foreign influences.

4

INDEPENDENCE UNDER THE HASMONEANS

In 201 B.C.E. the Seleucid king, Antiochus III, invaded Eretz Yisrael and defeated the army of the Ptolemies. At that time the Jewish leaders were fighting among themselves. They could not agree on whether to support the Ptolemies or the Seleucids. The group, headed by the High Priest, Simon the Just, supported the Seleucids. In return, Antiochus III granted them permission to live according to the laws of their forefathers.

Ten years later, Antiochus III set out on an expedition of conquest in Asia Minor and was defeated by his enemies—the Roman army. The Romans made the Seleucids pay them huge amounts of money. Because of this debt, the policy of the Selecuid kings toward the Jewish people changed for the worse. Antiochus III was killed while plundering a temple for its treasury, and his successor, Antiochus IV Epiphanes "The Great," also had to pay the outstanding debt to Rome.

At the same time, in Jerusalem, there was a struggle for the office of High Priest. Jason, brother of Onias III, the outgoing High Priest, knew how much the Seleucid king needed money, so he bought the office from him. By doing this, he broke the tradition of the high priesthood passing from father to son. He made it into an office which could be bought for money from the foreign ruler. Jason used his position to turn Jerusalem into a Hellenistic city by setting up Greek institutions of education, culture, and sports. Those who supported these changes were called Hellenists, and those who opposed them were called Hasideans (from the Hebrew word *hasid*, a God-fearing person).

Jason held the high priesthood for three years. He was followed by Menelaus, who also bought the office with money. With Menelaus' appointment, the office of High Priest was removed from the traditional family line of Zadok that had held the priesthood since the time of King Solomon.

Developing the body was an important part of Hellenistic culture. The photograph on the far left shows a painting of two wrestlers on a vase from ancient Greece.

In Maresha lived wealthy people who adopted the Hellenistic culture. Excavation there revealed tombs decorated by colored wall paintings such as the one in the picture on the left.

THE EDICTS OF ANTIOCHUS

Antiochus IV, like his father, wanted to conquer Egypt, which was under the rule of the Ptolemies. From 169 to 168 B.C.E., he led his army several times into Egypt. On returning from his first campaign he entered Jerusalem and plundered the Temple treasury. This greatly angered the people. During his second campaign in Egypt, false rumors that he had been killed reached Jerusalem, and riots broke out in the city.

Antiochus rushed back to Jerusalem to subdue the riots. A fortress, the Acra, was built south of the Temple Mount, and a Seleucid garrison was stationed there. Antiochus punished the rioters harshly.

A coin of Antiochus IV, right, with the king's head on one side, and Antiochus shown as the Greek god Zeus on the other side.

Center: The edicts of Antiochus led to martyrdom among the Jews. In a poem for Hanukkah, from a 15th-century manuscript, there are drawings describing the martyrdom. The drawing here shows Hannah watching her sons being put to death.

The Hanukkah lights are lit in memory of the cleansing of the Temple in 164 B.C.E. On the right are 18th- and 19th-century Hanukkah menorahs or candle-holders.

On the far right are clay lamps from the 1st and 2nd century B.C.E.

Several edicts were passed against the Jewish people: a statue of the Greek god Zeus and an altar for pagan worship were placed in the Temple; the Jews were forbidden to keep the commandments of the Torah, especially the observance of the Sabbath and circumcision; throughout Judah, shrines were built to Greek gods, Torah scrolls were burned, and anyone breaking the king's edicts could be put to death.

The Jews reacted to Antiochus' persecution in two ways. One was martyrdom, as in the story of Hannah and her seven sons, who refused to bow before the statue of Zeus, and were put to death. The other way was to fight Seleucid rule. Jews fleeing the cities to the Judean Desert set up a popular religious movement of rebellion, headed by the Hasideans.

The Hasmonean family, from the village of Modi'in, led the revolt. When the king's men came to enforce the edicts in their village, Mattathias the Hasmonean and his sons attacked them and then fled to the mountains. Most of the people supported them, and a small army of volunteers, mainly farmers, joined them. Soon after the revolt started,

Mattathias died and the leadership passed to his son Judah Maccabee (the name *Maccabee* came from the Hebrew word *makevet* which means "hammer"). First, the rebels cut off the Hellenizers and the Seleucid garrison in Jerusalem from the rest of the country under Seleucid control. The Seleucid army planned to attack the rebel's camp. However, Judah and his men used a very cunning tactic: they abandoned their camp as if in a panic and, while the Seleucid soldiers were searching for them in the mountains, they attacked the Seleucid camp and set it aflame. At this time, the commander of the Seleucids, Lysias, received news from home which made it necessary for him to return. As soon as he left the country, Judah took control of Jerusalem. The rebels could then cleanse the Temple of the pagan idols and renew holy worship there. This took place on the 25th of Kislev (December), 164 B.C.E., and is celebrated in the holiday of Hanukkah. (The word *hanukkah* means dedication, as in the dedication of the Temple.) The festivities lasted eight days. Ever since then, the festival of Hanukkah is celebrated by the Jews.

Meanwhile, Antiochus IV died, and the crown passed to his young son, Antiochus V. He canceled the edicts and allowed the rebels to keep their control of the Temple. But the fight was not yet over. The high priesthood was still in the hands of the Hellenizers, and Judah wanted to free his country completely from the Seleucids. Judah then gained a political victory which helped this. He sent a delegation to Rome, the Seleucid Kingdom's rival, who made a treaty with the Romans. This forced the Seleucids to try once more to put down the revolt. Judah Maccabee was slain in this battle.

REVOLT AND INDEPENDENCE
Jonathan, Judah's brother, became the next leader of the revolt. He continued to lead the army of the few in battle against the Seleucids and the Hellenizers. Independence, however, was won by political cunning. In Syria, a number of commanders were fighting for the throne, and each of them tried to win Jonathan's support. The one who succeeded was Alexander Balas, who held the throne for five years.

In 152 B.C.E. Jonathan was appointed High Priest, and in 150 B.C.E. he was appointed Governor of Judah. Judah was by now almost fully independent, but still had to pay taxes to the Seleucids. His appointment as High Priest, however, was not acceptable from a Jewish point of view, as it had been

made by a foreign ruler.

Jonathan was murdered by a Seleucid commander, who feared his growing power. The last surviving son of Mattathias, Simeon, became the leader. He made a treaty with the Seleucid king Demetrius II, under which Judah no longer had to pay any taxes. Judah was now an independent state, and Simeon became the religious, political, and military leader. In 140 B.C.E. an assembly of all the people, called the Great Assembly, gathered in Jerusalem and officially approved his

The Tombs of the Hasmoneans, believed by some people to be the Hasmoneans' burial place, are a series of sepulchers cut out of the rock near the Arab village of Al-Midya, identified as Modi'in.

23

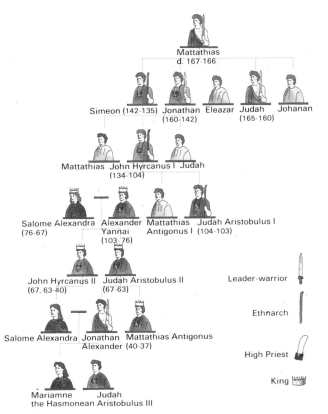

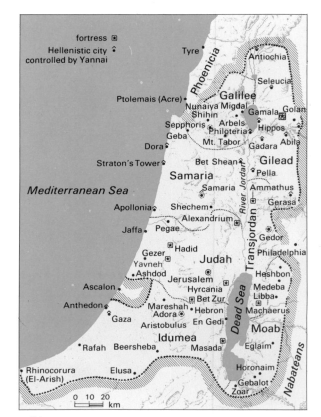

Tyre
Antiochia
Seleucia
Phoenicia
Galilee
Golan
Ptolemais (Acre)
Nunaiya Migdal
Shihin
Gamala
Sepphoris
Arbels
Philoteria
Hippos
Geba
Dora
Mt. Tabor
Gadara
Abila
Straton's Tower
Bet Shean
Gilead
Pella
Samaria
Mediterranean Sea
Samaria
Ammathus
Apollonia
Shechem
Gerasa
Jaffa
Pegae
Alexandrium
Transjordan
Gezer
Hadid
Judah
Philadelphia
Yavneh
Ashdod
Jerusalem
Heshbon
Ascalon
Hyrcania
Medeba
Anthedon
Mareshah
Bet Zur
Libba
Gaza
Adora
Hebron
Machaerus
Aristobulus
En Gedi
Idumea
Moab
Rafah
Beersheba
Masada
Eglaim
Rhinocorura
(El-Arish)
Elusa
Horonaim
Gebalot
Zoar
Nabateans
Dead Sea
River Jordan
0 10 20
km

Leader-warrior

Ethnarch

High Priest

King

*The Hasmoneans
(167–37 B.C.E.)*

*The map on the right
shows the Hasmonean
Kingdom at the time of
Yannai.*

high office. However, he was not able to pass his own laws and judge people according to them. For the "Law of the Forefathers" (Law of the Torah) was the law which ruled the land of Judah. Every Jew, even the head of state, was subject to that law. The Great Assembly also agreed that Simeon's office be passed on to his heirs after his death. This was how the Hasmonean dynasty began. It was a dynasty which ruled Judah for almost one hundred years, until it was conquered by Rome.

In order to strengthen his new state, Simeon made treaties with Sparta, in Greece, and with Rome. Now the kingdom was strong enough to stand up to the Seleucids. When they demanded that Simeon pay for the damage which the Jews caused in the war, he refused. The Seleucids were quite displeased, but it was not they who killed Simeon. The death blow came from within: Ptolemy, his son-in-law, wanted to be ruler of Judah. Encouraged by the Seleucid king, Antiochus VII, he laid a trap for Simeon and murdered him in 134 B.C.E. Two of his sons were also murdered with him. The attempt to overthrow the

Hasmonean dynasty, however, failed. The people and the army supported Simeon's son, John Hyrcanus, and appointed him their ruler and High Priest, just as they had done with his father.

John Hyrcanus ruled for thirty years, from 134 to 104 B.C.E. He made the independent state of Judah bigger, adding the Greek city-states and their surrounding villages throughout the land. His son, Judah Aristobulus, who only ruled for one year, extended these conquests.

The new ruler was Alexander Yannai, Judah Aristobulus' brother. He wanted his kingdom to reach as far as the Kingdom of David had, some 900 years earlier. He fought many wars in the course of his 27-year reign, and succeeded in reaching his goal. The many wars, his long absences from Jerusalem, the foreign customs which he brought into the Temple—all these things angered the Pharisees.

The Pharisees were descendants of the Hasideans from the days of the Hasmoneans. The word derives from the Hebrew word *parash* which means to be separated. The Pharisees were those who avoided others for reasons of ritual purity. They

24

demanded that Yannai give up the high priesthood. There was also another reason the people opposed him: he was the first Hasmonean ruler to take the title of king. In doing this he went against the decision of the people at the Great Assembly that had been made in the

days of Simeon the Hasmonean. The title of king, according to the Hellenistic meaning, gave him the power of lawmaker. This went against the Jewish view that laws came from the Bible.

A revolt broke out against Yannai, which he cruelly suppressed. Yannai's opponents were either imprisoned, or else fled the country. Nevertheless, during his long reign, Eretz Yisrael's trade flourished, and cities developed. Great wealth flowed into the hands of a few people. Many peasants suffered greatly from the wars in which they had to fight, and the heavy taxes they had to support.

Shortly before his death in 76 B.C.E., Yannai summoned his wife, Salome, and bequeathed her the crown. He advised her to turn to the support of the Pharisees, who were actually his opponents. The people

loved the queen. She freed the political prisoners, and scholars who had fled the land now returned. Since she herself could not serve as High Priest, her son John Hyrcanus filled this office. But his younger brother, Judah Aristobulus, did not think John Hyrcanus was fit to serve as both High Priest and king. As soon as their mother died, he went to war against his brother.

The Romans entered the war between the two brothers. The Roman commander, Pompey, had just arrived in Damascus, the Seleucid capital. Each of the brothers tried to gain Pompey's support but John Hyrcanus succeeded. Pompey invaded Jerusalem, which was then in the hands of Aristobulus, with great force in 63 B.C.E. Thus came about the end of the independent Kingdom of Judah.

Left: Tombs in the Kidron Valley near Jerusalem, dating from the Hasmonean period, were built by nobility to mark family graves. These tombs were built in the Hellenistic style, similar to the ones in Petra, shown above.
The Hellenistic-style burial palace in Petra (now in Jordan) was cut out of the rock. Petra was the capital of the Nabatean people, who lived in Hasmonean days in the southern part of Eretz Yisrael.

5

UNDER THE YOKE OF ROME

The Romans conquered the Land of Israel in 63 B.C.E. Judah lost most of the land that the Hasmoneans had captured, and also its independence. The title of king was taken from Hyrcanus. Because he was High Priest, he was still thought of as the leader of the Jews, but the ruler was now Antipater. He was the son of an Idumean family which had converted to Judaism. Antipater was appointed director of the affairs of the state by Julius Caesar. One of Antipater's sons, Herod, was appointed governor of the Galilee (47 B.C.E.).

However, the Hasmoneans did not give up. Mattathias Antigonus, grandson of Yannai, seized control of Judah. He was helped by the Parthians, who invaded Syria and also the Land of Israel during their wars against the Romans. Herod fled to Rome, where the Roman Senate appointed him King of Judah as a reward for his loyalty to the

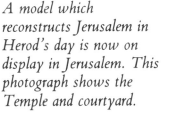

A model which reconstructs Jerusalem in Herod's day is now on display in Jerusalem. This photograph shows the Temple and courtyard.

Romans. Following his coronation, Herod set out for Eretz Yisrael at the head of an army. After a three-year war he seized control of Jerusalem, and Antigonus was put to death (37 B.C.E.).

HEROD'S KINGDOM

Herod enjoyed little support among the Jews. Most of them thought of him as an "Idumean servant" who did not deserve to have power. During the first few years of his rule, he was very busy suppressing rivals. Dozens of people, including many members of the Hasmonean family, were put to death and had their property taken away.

Herod wanted to turn his kingdom into part of the Roman Empire, and so he encouraged foreign influences. Many people who worked in the government and the army were not Jews. New cities were built which contained many Hellenistic-style buildings. Sebaste was built by Herod in 27 B.C.E. on the site of the city of Samaria. This was Herod's first major building project. He turned it into a garrison town, and trained the people who lived in it to serve him as soldiers.

Herod interfered in many ways with the Jewish tradition and way of life. He appointed and dismissed high priests, he ordered many executions, and he also practiced the "Law of Robbers"—meaning that thieves were sold into slavery to foreign countries—which was against the Jewish laws. All this, together with the heavy taxes which they had to pay, made the people very displeased with Herod's rule. Those who opposed him were punished with imprisonment and exile.

However, many Jews did find work on the huge building projects, and the large cities gave them a place to sell their produce. New roads were built, as well as the port town of Caesarea. The most important project was the building of the Temple. This was done strictly according to the Jewish ritual law.

Toward the end of his days, Herod placed a golden eagle, which was a Roman image, on the front of the Temple as a sign of his loyalty to Rome. This act made the people furious. Pharisee sages destroyed the image, and Herod, in one of his last acts before he died in 4 B.C.E., had

Jerusalem images of Caesar and had them attached to the poles of the Roman legions—which was against the Jewish religion. He also used the Temple's treasury for building projects, and it was he who ordered the crucifixion of Jesus.

THE GREAT REVOLT

Since the time of the Roman occupation, the Jewish people had never stopped longing for the end of foreign rule. Under the rule of the procurator Antonius Felix (52–60 C.E.) the Jewish rebels, known as "zealots," became very active. Sometimes they would attack fellow Jews whom they thought were collaborating with the Romans.

them put to death. In these difficult times, many people started to believe in the coming days of freedom from distress, and several extremist religious sects sprang up. This is also the time when Jesus lived.

After Herod's death, his son, Archelaus, ruled over Judah. He was very cruel and the people despised him. They complained frequently to the Romans. Eventually Archelaus was removed, and Judah was made into a Roman province, called Judea. From 6 to 66 C.E. Judea was ruled by officers of the Roman Empire, called procurators. The harshest of these was Pontius Pilate. He brought into

These zealots were called *sicarii*, from the Latin word *sica*, or curved dagger, which they used.

On Passover in 66 C.E., when many Jews were in Jerusalem to celebrate the festival, Roman soldiers burst into the city, plundered and murdered, and robbed the Temple of its treasures. The Jews fought back forcefully, and many lost their lives. The rebellion turned into open war. The priests decided to refuse to make the sacrifice in the Temple in honor of the Roman Caesar. The rebels seized control of the Temple area, conquered a nearby fortress and

Rows of pillars, which lead to the town of Sebaste, are shown in the photograph at left.

Above: Jewish captives carrying the Holy Lamp (the Menorah) and other treasures of the Temple are sculpted in the triumphal arch in Rome, which was built in honor of Titus' victory.

In the Roman coin above, which bears the inscription "Judea Capta," Judah is shown as a humbled Jewish figure sitting under a palm tree, and standing over the figure is an armed Roman soldier.

Masada, below right, is in the Judean desert, on a cliff overlooking the Dead Sea. This was the last Jewish fortress to fall into Roman hands in 73 C.E.

Below is a picture of Rabban Gamliel from a Haggadah, probably from Crete, 1583. Rabban means "our master" in Hebrew. It was a title given to the head of the Sanhedrin.

wiped out the Roman garrison stationed there. The revolt soon spread all over the country. In Rome, Caesar Nero sent Vespasian, his best commander, to crush the revolt. Vespasian gathered an army of 60,000 men and set out for Judea. One by one, all the towns fell under his control. Only then did the Romans turn to Jerusalem.

In Jerusalem the rebel forces were quarrelling among themselves for control of the city. During this civil war the city's food supplies were burned.

In the meantime Vespasian had become Caesar of the Roman Empire. He sent his son Titus to Judea, to put an end to the war. In 70 C.E. the Romans began their attack. The strong city walls made conquering Jerusalem difficult, but the citizens were weak from hunger. After fifteen days the Romans managed to enter the city easily. On the ninth day of the month of Av (July) the Romans conquered the Temple Mount, broke into the Temple, and set it aflame. For the Jewish people this remains a day of mourning for the destruction of the Temple.

The results of the defeat were disastrous. Thousands died on the battlefield. Many others, including the rebel leaders, were captured and taken to Rome as prisoners. Even after the fall of Jerusalem, groups of zealots continued to fight. Three strongholds remained in their hands—Herodium, Machaerus and Masada. Herodium and Machaerus soon fell. The sicarii made their stand in Masada under the command of Eleazar, son of Yair. The Romans laid siege to Masada. The rebels held out for about one year, but the Romans built a ramp up the side of the mountain and broke through the first wall with a battering ram. Then they set fire to the second wall. When the rebels saw that they stood no chance, they all decided to take their own lives rather than fall into the hands of the Romans. The Romans attached much importance to putting down the Great Revolt in Judah. This can be seen from the huge number of coins that the Roman Empire minted in honor of its victory. They bear the inscription "Judea Taken Captive" (*Judea Capta* in Latin). The coins, as they passed from hand to hand, served to publicize the victory.

The fall of Jerusalem took away the heart of Jewish religious and spiritual life. Some of the nation's leaders had died in the revolt, and others were forced into hiding. One of the few leaders who could act openly was Yohanan, son of Zakkai. This was because he had not supported the revolt. Before the fall of Jerusalem he had served in the Sanhedrin, or Great Assembly, which was the religious, legal, and lawmaking body for the Jews. In the last stages of the siege of Jerusalem, Yohanan somehow managed to escape. After the fall of Jerusalem a group of sages gathered in Yavneh, and together with Yohanan they again set up the Sanhedrin. But many people were against Yohanan because he had fled from Jerusalem. This finally caused him to step down. Leadership passed into the hands of Rabban Gamliel, grandson

of the leader of the Sanhedrin before the revolt. Unlike Yohanan, Rabban Gamliel was very popular with the Jews in Eretz Yisrael and in other countries. They all lived according to the rules laid down in Yavneh by the Tannaim, the sages who explained the Biblical laws. One of the most important was the rite of prayers in the synagogue, three times a day.

THE BAR KOKHBA REVOLT

Although the crushing of the Great Revolt brought ruin and destruction upon the Jewish people, it also gave birth to new movements. The Jewish leaders tried to convince the people to accept the Roman rulers in order to survive. But many continued to hope for the defeat of Rome and the coming of the Messiah, which would free them from the Romans and bring about the rebuilding of the Temple.

In 130 C.E. Caesar Hadrian visited Eretz Yisrael. Two of his acts struck at the very heart of Judaism. First, he forbade the Jews to practice circumcision, and then he began to rebuild Jerusalem as a Roman city. He changed its name to Aelia Capitolina and planned a temple to Zeus at its center. The Jews viewed these acts against their religion as being worse than death.

The revolt broke out in the summer of 132 C.E.. It was led by Simeon, son of Kosiba. Some of the sages supported him, the most important being Rabbi Akiva. (The title *rabbi* means "my master," or "teacher," and is given to those who have trained to be religious leaders.) It is written that when Rabbi Akiva saw Simeon, he said: "There shall come a star (*kokhav*) out of Jacob." From then on, Simeon was known as Bar Kokhba—Son of a Star. Rabbi Akiva also called him "King Messiah." Bar Kokhba organized the revolt secretly, in caves in the Judean Desert. The preparations the

Silver coins from the time of the Bar Kokhba revolt. The words inscribed on them read: "For the Freedom of Jerusalem," and "For the Redemption of Israel." The symbols on the coins, and also on the goblets used in the Temple worship, all express the rebels' hopes for freedom and the coming of the Messiah.

Cave entrances pocketing the cliff in the Judean Desert, where the rebels took refuge.

The photograph below shows copper household wares used by the Bar Kokhba rebels, found in one of the caves.

Jews made for the revolt are described by the Roman historian Dio Cassius (2nd–3rd century): "They seized the well-situated locations in the country, and fortified them with trenches and walls, to serve them as places of refuge and also to allow them to move about secretly. They bored openings into the underground passages to let in air and light."

The revolt broke out suddenly

29

A bracket which supported the roof made of stone and decorated with a palm tree (above), and a chariot carved in the form of a temple with a holy ark (above right), from a synagogue at Capernaum, in the Galilee, dating from the 3rd century.

Bet She'arim, on the right, in the Galilee, was built in Hasmonean times, but the town flourished especially during the time of Judah ha-Nasi. Catacombs from the 2nd–4th centuries C.E. were found there. This photograph shows the elaborate entrances to the tombs.

Bet Shean, then called Scythopolis or Nissa, was a mixed town, where both Jews and non-Jews lived. This Roman theater was built there in the third century.

and with great force. It took the Romans completely by surprise. The Romans failed to overcome Bar Kokhba and the rebels, and Jerusalem fell into their hands.

Because the rebels caused so much damage to the Roman garrison in Judea, Hadrian decided to take strong action. He called in his senior commander, Julius Severus, the governor of Britain. Giving him a large army, he told him to take command of the war. Severus' forces cut off the rebel strongholds and villages from each other until, one by one, they were captured. Many of the rebels died in caves. The Romans besieged them for a very long time, leaving them without food or water. Hundreds of thousands died in battle. Tens of thousands were sold into slavery. Judea was almost completely emptied of Jews. The Romans changed the name of Judea to Syria-Palestina, and Jerusalem, now a Roman colony, was settled with gentiles. Jews were forbidden even to enter the city.

The center of Jewish life moved from Judea to the Galilee, in the northern part of the country, which had not suffered in the revolt. There the sages again set about rebuilding the ruins of Jewish life. Many synagogues were built there. As in Yavneh, rules were once more laid down regarding Jewish life in Eretz Yisrael and in other countries in the Diaspora. Judah ha-Nasi ("the President"), grandson of Rabban Gamliel of Yavneh, served as head of the Sanhedrin from around 185–220. He was very popular, and the people called him simply "Rabbi." The most important thing that Rabbi did was to bring together all the traditions of the Oral Laws into one book called the Mishnah (from the Hebrew word *shinun* meaning "teaching" or "repetition"). Out of the Mishnah grew another great work—the Talmud, a commentary and discussions on the Mishnah. The death of Rabbi Judah ha-Nasi, like his life, was very significant to the Jewish people. They saw his death as the end of a chapter in Jewish history.

6

ERETZ YISRAEL FROM ONE CONQUEROR TO THE NEXT

At the end of the third century, the Roman Empire broke up and was split into two—the Western Roman Empire with Rome at its center, and the Eastern Roman Empire, called Byzantium. Its capital was the city of Constantinople (today in Turkey). Byzantium ruled over Eretz Yisrael from the years 324 to 640, when the country was conquered by the Arabs.

UNDER BYZANTINE RULE

Christianity, which began in Eretz Yisrael, spread throughout the Roman Empire. For many years the Roman rulers persecuted the Christians. However, the Byzantine king Constantine the Great, who converted to Christianity himself, recognized Christianity as the official religion in the year 313. Constantine conquered Eretz Yisrael and joined it to the Byzantine Empire, thus becoming its first Christian ruler. He allowed his Jewish subjects to keep their religion, but they were forbidden to marry Christians or to keep slaves, in case they converted them to Judaism. Throughout Eretz Yisrael, especially in Bethlehem and

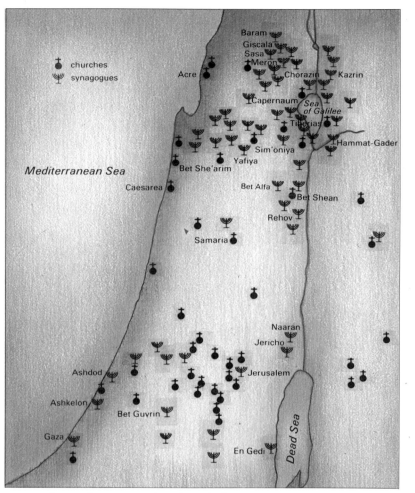

Jerusalem, large and splendid churches were built which attracted many Christian pilgrims. As the number of Christians grew, new churches and many monasteries were built.

Life for the Jews of Eretz Yisrael became hard. The leaders of the

Synagogues and churches in Eretz Yisrael in the Byzantine era are shown on this map.

The Monastery of Santa Caterina in the Sinai desert, far left. Built in the 6th century, it is named after Catherine of Alexandria, who died a martyr's death in the early 4th century for protesting against persecution of the Christians.

On the left is a font for holy water cut from a single stone and shaped like a cross, which was found in a church at Shivta in the Negev.

Right: Part of the mosaic floor from a 6th century synagogue discovered at Bet Alfa. In the outer circle are the 12 signs of the zodiac. In the center is a figure of the sun god in a chariot harnessed to four horses. In the corners are the four seasons represented by winged female figures. Mosaic floors similar in style were also found in churches.

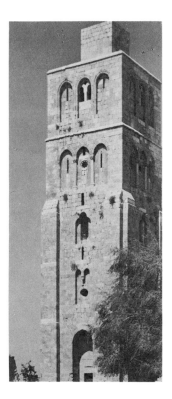

"The White Mosque" in Ramlah is so named for its color. Construction of the mosque began during the Ummayad Caliphates, and it was completed hundreds of years later in the 15th century.

Part of an illuminated manuscript of the Bible from the year 929, top right, which was apparently written in Tiberias. The drawing describes the temple and its vessels.

Church were against them. Jews were forbidden to enter Jerusalem, except on the anniversary of the destruction of the Temple—on the 9th day of Av. They were harassed by the Christians, even though it was against the law. Many Jews left the country. Those who remained kept up their active community life, as we can see by the many beautiful synagogues that were built during this time.

Despite their hardships, Jews throughout the Empire were kept together for generations by the Sanhedrin of Eretz Yisrael. The presidents of the Sanhedrin, descendants of the House of David, had great authority. Their emissaries influenced the appointment of the leaders of the different Jewish communities.

The Church did its best to destroy their power. It succeeded around the year 425 when the presidency of the Sanhedrin was especially weak. This marked the end of a dynasty which had stood at the head of the Jewish nation for at least 350 years. Synagogues were also thought of as strengthening the community, so laws were passed by the Byzantine kings forbidding the building of new synagogues. More Jews left Eretz Yisrael, and by the 6th century the Christians became the majority.

For a very short period at the beginning of the 7th century, the Sassanid Persian Empire conquered and took over Eretz Yisrael from the Byzantines. Many Jews, mainly from the Galilee, joined the Persian fighters. They had suffered under the Christian Byzantine rule and hoped to gain self-rule. But the Persians were defeated and thrown out of the country. Many Jews were executed or forced to renounce their religion. So by the time the Arab conquerors arrived a few years later, the Jews received them with open arms.

UNDER ARAB RULE

The Arabs set out on expeditions of conquest in the Arabian Peninsula in 634. Within 100 years they had conquered all of the Middle East and North Africa, and their domain extended as far as Tibet in the Far East and Spain in the west. In 638 they took Jerusalem, and two years later turned Eretz Yisrael into a part of the Umayyad Caliphate (kingdom).

The first Muslim Caliph (a Muslim king) in Eretz Yisrael allowed seventy Jewish families to settle in Jerusalem, for the first time since the defeat of Bar Kokhba in 135. A new city, Ramlah, was built on the sand (*raml* is Arabic for "sand") along the coastal Via Maris,

32

Tiberias was thought of as the continuation of the Sanhedrin.

The Umayyad Caliphate was centered in Damascus, Syria, not far from Eretz Yisrael. Therefore the country was considered to be an important province, and under their rule it enjoyed peace and security. The Umayyads rebuilt the coastal towns and developed Jerusalem. But in 750 the Abbasid family came to power, and made Baghdad (today in Iraq) their capital. The rulers gave

Below: An illuminated manuscript of the book of Numbers from Egypt, dating from the 12th century.

the Exilarch, the leader of the Jewish exiles in Babylonia (Iraq today), authority over all the Jews in the Arab empire—from Persia in the east to Spain in the west. Alongside him were the heads of the great Babylonian Jewish Academies, or *Yeshivot*. They bore the title of *gaon* ("a very wise man" in Hebrew), and they were the spiritual leaders of the whole Jewish nation. Thus the spiritual center was moved from Eretz Yisrael to Babylonia. The Abbasid dynasty's decline began in the 9th century, as bands of the Shi'ite Muslim sect overran Syria and Eretz Yisrael. With the increased unrest, many Jews left Eretz Yisrael for Egypt.

A new Muslim dynasty which rose to power in Egypt—the Fatimids—took control over Eretz Yisrael in 969. Cairo was made the capital, and the Jewish community there became prosperous. Archives of Jewish manuscripts from the 9th century were found in the Ezra

The two photographs above left are of Hisham's Palace in Jericho, assumed to have been built in the days of the Caliph Walid II (743–744). Above top left: A mosaic on the wall of the council-chamber of the palace. To the left of the abundant tree are deer grazing peacefully, and on the right is a deer being preyed upon by a lion. Above left center: Carved stone pillars of one of the walls of the palace. The palace was destroyed in an earthquake in 746.

The Pool of St. Helena, above at left, built by the Caliph Harun al-Rashid in Ramlah at the end of the 8th century.

and from the outset was planned as a trading, industrial, and administrative city.

Caliph Suleiman and his successors put great energy into developing the city, building a magnificent palace and mosque, water reservoirs, and apparently even a surrounding wall. Building lots were offered to potential settlers in the city. The Jewish community in the town of Ramlah was extremely prosperous, and sometimes even overshadowed Jerusalem. The Jewish religious and cultural center at that time was Tiberias in the Galilee. The Jewish Academy (*Yeshivah* in Hebrew) of

33

Synagogue in Cairo. In these archives, members of the community stored ritual objects, holy scriptures, hymns, and documents, after they were torn and worn out. The archives were discovered at the end of the 19th century and from the documents found there, one can learn much about the life of the Jews from different communities over hundreds of years.

The Fatimids preferred the Jews to the Christians, and sometimes even to their Muslim rivals. At this time the Jewish Academy moved back from Tiberias to Jerusalem, and the number of Jews in the city grew. They made their living from donations which came from Jewish communities in the Diaspora.

Due to the weakness of the Fatimid government, Muslim tribes took over parts of Eretz Yisrael and attacked the inhabitants. The number of Jews in Jerusalem decreased, Jewish pilgrims stopped coming, and as a result donations ceased. By the time of the Crusader invasion of Eretz Yisrael, only a few thousand Jews were left.

THE CRUSADERS IN ERETZ YISRAEL

The First Crusade set out from Europe for the Land of Israel in 1096. Its aim was to liberate the grave of Jesus from the "Muslim Infidels." The Crusaders attacked the Jewish communities they encountered along their way, and this frightened both the Jews and Muslims of Eretz Yisrael. Therefore when the Crusaders entered Ramlah and Jaffa in 1099, they found these cities deserted. The Crusaders besieged Jerusalem, then entered the city and murdered most of the people. Jews who were taken prisoner and sold into slavery were ransomed by Jews from various communities. The Crusaders forbade non-Christians to live in the city. Jerusalem was once more emptied of Jews.

The Crusaders took over all of

The Crusaders built many churches in Eretz Yisrael. In the photograph above, part of a carved wall with figures of Christian saints, from the Church of the Annunciation in Nazareth, built in the 12th and 13th centuries. The carving was done in the style popular in the Crusaders' home countries.

A battle between the Crusaders and the Muslims—an illustration, above center, from a 14th-century manuscript. The Christian knights have shields and helmets with the sign of the cross. The Muslims, wearing eastern-style clothes with the sign of the crescent, have drawn swords only.

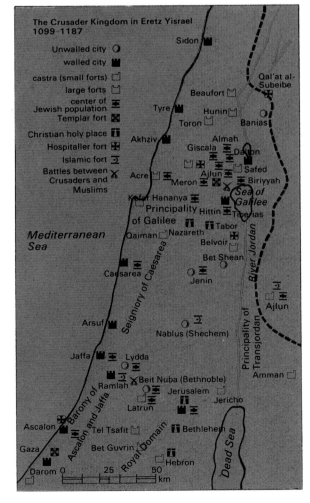

The Crusader Kingdom in Eretz Yisrael
1099-1187

Eretz Yisrael, and established a kingdom which lasted until 1110. The constant threat from the Muslims, the desire to rule over large areas, and the lack of manpower—all of this caused the Crusaders to build forts, castles, and fortifications throughout the country. The Crusaders depended on the local inhabitants to work for them and pay them taxes, so they let them stay in the conquered towns and villages. These people, including the Jews, were allowed to live according to their own customs. But the Academy (Yeshivah) of Eretz Yisrael—the most important Jewish institution, which had moved some hundred years before from Jerusalem to Tyre—now moved from Tyre, which had been conquered by the Crusaders, to Damascus. It never came back to Eretz Yisrael.

In 1187 the city of Jerusalem was captured by the Muslim conqueror Saladin. During this time Jews began to settle again in Jerusalem, although the city—which in the 13th century was an unwalled city—was not a safe place to live, and this discouraged people from settling there. In 1260 Rabbi Moses Nachmanides (the Ramban), one of the great interpreters of Jewish law, arrived in Jerusalem—after fleeing from the Christians in Spain. This is what he wrote to his son about the city: "Israel is gone from the city, save for two brothers who bought a dyeing concession from the ruler."

The Ramban established a synagogue and brought the Torah scrolls back to the city. But he never succeeded in reviving a real Jewish community there.

The Jewish community in Acre, on the other hand, flourished during the 13th century. This town served as the capital of the second Crusader kingdom, which was established in the years 1191–1291. The Ramban lived there for the last three years of his life and gathered many pupils around him. The Ramban used to stress that: "Settlement in Eretz Yisrael outweighs all the commandments and is the duty of every generation." And indeed in the 13th century hundreds of Jews from Europe settled in the country.

In the spring of 1291, the Muslim Mamelukes conquered Acre, bringing to an end the Crusader rule. The Mameluke Sultan, who stood at the head of the conquering forces, ordered a massacre to avenge the killings by the Crusaders when they had conquered Jerusalem. Many Jews were among the victims. To prevent a new invasion from Europe, the Mamelukes destroyed all the coastal towns, and the inhabitants— including the Jews—were forced to live further inland. With the end of Crusader rule, Jewish settlement reached a new low level, and many years were to pass before it would recover.

Saladin (1137–1193)— the Crusaders' arch-foe— in a Persian miniature, above far left.

Above: The seal of Rabbi Moses Nahmanides (the Ramban), 1194–1270, found near Acre.

7

ON THE BANKS OF THE NILE AND IN BABYLONIA

In the first picture below, the ruins of the city of Yeb are on the right.

The second picture below shows the varied occupations of the Jews of Alexandria. Through writings from those days, we know that they made their living from trade, agriculture, crafts, and weaving, and there were also tax-collectors and ship owners. The drawing is done in the style of the ancient period.

Jews lived in Egypt, to the south of Eretz Yisrael, and in Babylonia, to the east, from the end of the period of the First Temple and after its destruction by the Assyrians in 586 B.C.E. Most of those who went to Egypt emigrated because of persecution and harsh economic conditions. The Jews went to Babylonia mainly because they had been exiled there by conquerors. In both these countries the Jewish communities grew until, after the Great Revolt and the Bar Kokhba Revolt, at the end of the 2nd century, there were more Jews living in those countries than in Eretz Yisrael.

ON THE BANKS OF THE NILE
Evidence of a renewed Jewish life in Egypt, on the banks of the Nile, can be learned from the fate of the Prophet Jeremiah. He himself, and others with him, left Jerusalem for Egypt after the city fell to the Babylonians. Papyri found in Yeb, a city built on an island on the southern border of Egypt, opposite Aswan, tell us about Jewish soldiers who lived there in the 5th century B.C.E., when Egypt was under Persian rule. The garrison there consisted of people of many nationalities, including Jews. Many other Jews lived there too, and they all enjoyed religious freedom. They even built a Temple there.

As a result of Alexander the Great's conquests in the East in 332 B.C.E., many Jews settled in Alexandria, the new city he had constructed in Egypt. Under the Ptolemaic dynasty, which came after Alexander, Egypt and Eretz Yisrael were united into one country for 130 years, and once more the Jewish community in Egypt grew.

Emigration continued after Judah came under Seleucid rule. Antiochus IV Epiphanes, the enemy of the Ptolemies, passed laws against the Jews which led to the Hasmonean uprising, and many more Jews emigrated as a result. The Ptolemies allowed the Jews to practice their religion freely. At the end of the 3rd century B.C.E., a Temple was built at Leontopolis, on the delta of the Nile.

Alexandria, a large port city, had a flourishing Jewish community. In the first century C.E. the population of Alexandria was a million, and the

Jews made up about 40% of it. The Jews kept their religion apart from the other inhabitants, held high government positions, and became prosperous.

All this caused both Greeks and Egyptians to become hostile to them. When Egypt became a Roman province, the hatred increased because the local residents thought that the rulers favored the Jews. In 38 C.E. Agrippas I, grandson of Herod and descendant of the Hasmoneans, was appointed king by the Roman Caesar of part of Judah. On his way to Eretz Yisrael he passed through Alexandria and the Jews gave him a royal welcome. This infuriated the other residents. They suspected the loyalty of the local Jews. Riots broke out, synagogues were burned down, shops were looted, and many Jews were murdered. The survivors were forced to live in one quarter—which was in fact the first ghetto.

Peace returned to the city after about two years, but not for long. When the Great Revolt broke out in Eretz Yisrael (66 C.E.), the Jews of Alexandria rebelled against the Romans. Once more riots broke out and thousands of Jews were killed.

Tension between the Jews of Egypt and their Roman rulers grew again about fifty years later, when the Roman army set out on a new war in the East. Jewish uprisings broke out in Egypt, in Cyrene (Libya today), and in Cyprus, and continued for about two years until

they were forcefully suppressed by the Emperor Trajanus in 117 C.E.

About a hundred years passed and, near the end of the 3rd century, the Jewish community once again recovered. But there were quarrels between Jews and Christians in Alexandria which resulted in the expulsion of the Jews from the city, in the year 415. In other towns, however, they carried on their lives without oppression, paying taxes to the rulers.

In the beginning of the 7th century,

Egypt was conquered by the Arabs. They united all the Jews in Spain, North Africa, Egypt, Eretz Yisrael, and Babylonia under one rule. From then on, Babylonia became the leading Jewish community.

BETWEEN THE RIVERS IN BABYLONIA

The area between the Euphrates and the Tigris rivers, which in ancient times was named Mesopotamia (Iraq today), was called Babylonia by the Jews. This name came from the kingdom of Babylon, which ruled the region when the Jews were

A clay lamp from Egypt, left, from the 4th century, with figures of David (on the right) and Goliath.

A bronze lamp from Egypt, left, from the 4th century. The menorah, a popular Jewish symbol, is engraved on it.

The Septuagint was the first translation of the Hebrew Bible. According to legend, it was translated into Greek by seventy men, hence its name. The translation was made for the Greek-speaking Jews. The Pentateuch was apparently completed by the 3rd century B.C.E., and was circulated from Egypt throughout the Jewish communities in the Hellenistic world. The page on the far left is from a 4th-century manuscript found at the Santa Catherina Monastery, in Sinai.

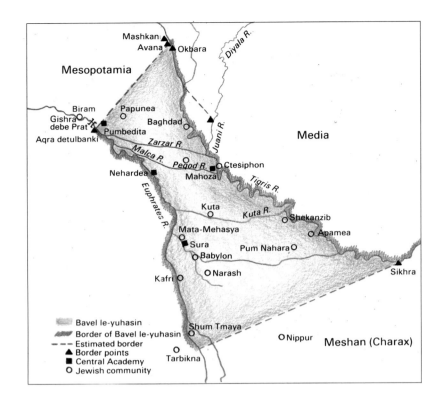

tailoring. They led their lives according to their religion, built synagogues, and, in the larger communities, they established Torah Academies, or Yeshivot, where they studied the Mishnah (the Oral Torah). Many people came to these

On the map:
The Jewish community of Babylonia.

In Dura Europos, a city on the Euphrates, the remains of a synagogue from the 2nd century were found. Its walls were covered with frescoes portraying figures and events from the Bible. In the picture above right, we see part of a fresco, showing Aaron the Priest, the Temple sanctuary, and its vessels.

A page from the Babylonian Talmud, right, printed in Venice, 1520–1527. This edition was the basis for all later editions. In the center is the Mishna written in Hebrew (in bolder lettering). The discussions of the Amoraim are written in Aramaic. In the margins are additional commentaries.

exiled there. Mesopotamia was later ruled by many kingdoms—the Persians, the Seleucids, the Parthians, the Persian Sassanids, and the Arabs. Little is known about Jewish life in Babylonia from the time the Jews were allowed to return to Judah in the 6th century B.C.E., to the 2nd century C.E., when the Parthians captured the area. The Parthian kings, like the Persians before them, allowed the Jews to live their lives according to their customs. The Persian Sassanids, who conquered Babylonia at the beginning of the 3rd century, and the Arabs, who conquered it at the beginning of the 7th century, also did not interfere with the Jews' way of life. The Jewish leadership recognized the new rulers and accepted the law of the land; as one sage said: "The law of the state is the law."

The Jews of Babylonia were spread across many towns between the Euphrates and the Tigris rivers. The more prestigious families lived in the region known as "Bavel le-yuhasin."

Most of the Jews in Babylonia were farmers. Other common occupations were trading and crafts such as pottery-making, tanning, and

Yeshivot during two months of the year—one month in the summer and one month in the winter—when there was little agricultural work to be done. They came to study with the sages, who were called the *amoraim* (from the Aramaic word *amora*—spokesman or interpreter). The Amoraim dealt with all the aspects of Jewish thought—spiritual as well as legal. Their writings, spanning over 300 years, were collected in the 6th century into the Babylonian Talmud. The sages who stood at the head of the great Yeshivot after the revising of the Talmud, when the country was conquered by the Muslims, were called *Geonim* (from the Hebrew word *Gaon*—a very wise person). They served as the spiritual leaders of almost all the world Jewish community. The Geonim kept close ties with the Jewish communities in other countries and sent thousands of

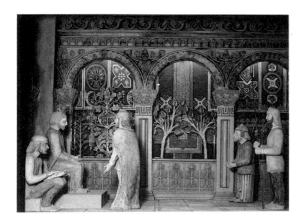

answers to questions which they received on different aspects of Jewish life. They also chose leaders of communities.

Alongside the heads of the Academies, who were the spiritual leaders, stood the Leaders in Exile, called Exilarchs. They filled many roles and had much power. They represented the Jews before the non-Jewish rulers, appointed the heads of the Academies and the judges, saw to the punishment of lawbreakers, and were in charge of funds. Their authority reached even beyond the borders of Babylonia. Thus, for example, Benjamin of Tudela, who traveled in the 12th century from one Jewish community to the other, wrote that on his journeys he visited distant communities, from Yemen to India, which were under the authority of the Exilarch.

From the period of the First Temple, when the Babylonians allowed the Jews to return to Jerusalem, there were strong links between Babylonia and Eretz Yisrael. However, from the 4th century on, there was competition between these two Jewish centers. They each wanted to be the leader of the Jewish communities in the Diaspora and to receive the most donations from them. Gradually, the Academies of Babylonia gained the

upper hand, and by the 10th century they enjoyed leadership of all the world Jewish communities.

However, it was at this time that these Academies started to lose their power, for two main reasons: Firstly, the Arab Muslim Caliphate had been divided into small Muslim kingdoms, and the rulers of these kingdoms were not in favor of the ties between their Jewish subjects and their rivals in Iraq. The second reason was that the Academies, or Yeshivot, turned into closed professional institutions, where ceremony was very important and sons inherited their fathers' positions, even if they were not suitable. There was little academic growth and development. In the course of the 11th century new, more vital centers of Torah study emerged in other parts of the world, and ties with the Babylonian Yeshivot grew weaker.

The Exilarchs considered themselves descendants of the House of David, which gave them the legal right to rule over the Jewish people. They built themselves a magnificent palace and ruled in the manner of kings. The photograph, far left, shows a model of the Exilarch in his court.

Quarrels between the Exilarch and the Geonim over the right of leadership sometimes needed to be settled by the Muslim authorities. The painting on the left shows the Caliph mediating in a dispute between Rav Sa'adiah Gaon and the Leader in Exile, David, son of Zakkai.

Aramaic was the spoken language of the Jews of Babylonia in the first few centuries C.E. This bowl, above, from Nippur (6th century), bears Aramaic inscriptions.

8

IN THE CHRISTIAN KINGDOMS OF EUROPE

These statues (below far right) stand in a 13th-century church in Germany. Unlike the proud figure of Ecclesia, on the left, Synagoga's eyes are covered and the Tablets of the Law she holds are upside down. This stands for the blindness of the Jews, which prevents them from seeing the truth.

In the center is a 13th-century illustration of a German king beheading a man who has killed a Jew. In paintings from this period, Jews are shown wearing bell-shaped caps, or marks of disgrace on their clothes. This was meant to set the Jews apart from the Christians.

The emigration, or rather exile, of Jews from Eretz Yisrael to the west grew when the Romans ruled the area. Jewish families grouped together to form communities in Asia Minor, Greece, and Italy, and even reached as far west as France, Germany, and Spain.

During the Middle Ages (7th–15th centuries), there were two powerful forces which controlled the status and conditions of the Jews: the local rulers and the Catholic Church. Although there were differences from place to place, the principle was the same everywhere. The rulers, whether they were kings or princes or local governors, all wanted Jews to live under their rule. Crafts developed and trade spread wherever Jews lived, mainly because they had close ties with the Jewish communities in other countries.

When the church forbade the

protection, and freedom to live as they wished.

The Catholic Church was a dominant force in Europe from the 7th century on. For the Catholic Church, the Jews were proof of the truth of Christianity. They had been the Chosen People before Jesus, but because of their refusal to believe in him and his disciples, their special status had been passed to the Christians. According to the Catholic Church, this was why the Jews living in Christian countries were now in such a poor state. One of the means used by the Church to display to the public the Jewish mistake was that of symbolic sculptures. Ecclesia and Synagoga, female figures representing Christianity and Judaism, were popular subjects in medieval Christian art. They tell us how Ecclesia (the Church), is superior to

Above: Satan binds the eyes of a Jew and together they try to corrupt pious Christians. This picture is a 14th-century illustration from France.

Christians to loan money, the Jews became moneylenders. The money they loaned or paid as taxes was an important source of income for the treasury of the rulers. They were perceived as the servant of the royal treasury, and whoever harmed them was thought of as harming the ruler's property. Thus they enjoyed

Synagoga. It was very important to the Church to convert as many Jews as possible to Christianity, in order to prove its superiority. To persuade them to convert, the Church tempted them with money and forced them to listen to the sermons of priests and monks and to take part in public debates in which they had to defend their faith. In those days the Church was against using force in order to convert the Jews. Under these conditions the Jews could usually keep up their lively and active community life.

The attitude toward the Jews during the Middle Ages was also influenced by the people themselves. However, it is difficult to speak of a single and uniform attitude toward the Jews on the part of farmers, townspeople, and nobles in Western Europe. In the 7th to 11th centuries, relations between Jews and non-Jews were quite close, and therefore the Church repeatedly warned against such contacts. These relations worsened at a later stage, particularly due to business reasons: the rise of local merchants who were afraid of Jewish competition; the money which had to be paid to moneylenders in interest on loans;

and the wish to cancel debts to these Jewish moneylenders. In addition, Church propaganda which accused the Jews of being responsible for the death of Jesus added to the bad feeling. The monarchy tried to stop the spreading of false accusations against the Jews.

However, as religious feeling became stronger and the central government became weaker, violence spread and thousands of victims were killed.

THE JEWISH COMMUNITY
The term "community" (kehillah in Hebrew) is generally used to describe an organized Jewish population that lived in a town or city alongside the local population. The activities of these communities varied from place to place and from time to time, but there were three major issues with which the Jewish community always dealt:

1. *Looking after religious needs.* To

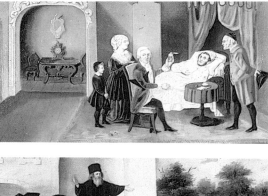

do this, the community established different types of institutions: synagogues, cemeteries, ritual baths, and courts. The Jewish court ruled in matters of personal status as well as crimes. Punishment was usually a fine, but sometimes the condemned were also sentenced to whipping or imprisonment. Those who did not

The wooden synagogue of Zabludow in Poland, shown below far left. It was built in the 18th century and was burned down in the Second World War.

Visiting and aiding the sick was one of the most important commandments of Judaism. The painting at left is from Prague in the 18th century.

The fortified synagogue of Lutsk in Poland, below, was built in 1626. Such synagogues were built outside the city walls as defense posts in case of enemy attack.

In Judaism burial of the dead is called "an act of true kindness." This important commandment is carried out by volunteers. The painting of a funeral, in the center above left, is from 18th-century Prague.

A Jewish court, above left. At the head stood the president of the court and at his side, the judges. Before him stood the accused and the public. The picture comes from a book of 15th-century Italy.

Ages and spoken by some Ashkenazi Jews to this day.

The first Jewish communities in Ashkenaz arose on the trade routes along the Rhine, the Danube, and the Elbe rivers. The Jews at this time made their living mainly from trade. The non-Jews of that time

A Jewish moneylender is shown above at top in a German engraving from the 16th century.

"Jews at the Stake," above right, is an illumination from a 14th-century Belgian manuscript. The Jews were accused of poisoning the wells and rivers.

A deer is chased by a hunter in a painting from the 15th century, shown in the above illumination. The deer trapped within the circle stands for Jewry persecuted by the Christians.

The drawing above far right, from a prayerbook of the 14th century, shows a boy who is just beginning to study the Torah (on the left) being offered candies.

carry out the punishment were threatened with excommunication (banishment from the community).

2. *Aiding the needy.* Here the main institutions were the charity fund and soup kitchen.

3. *Defense and security of life and property.* For this, the people paid a tax, each according to his own means. Where Jews lived in closed quarters, the community was responsible for sanitation, inspection of housing, and posting of guards at the gate.

The community also played an important role in educating the children. It maintained a *heder,* where the child began his formal education at the age of four, and a Yeshivah, where he later studied the Torah and Talmud.

The community was run by a small committee whose members were known as the heads, elders, or aldermen of the city. There was a council responsible for setting laws, making decisions, and electing the heads of the community. Several large Jewish populations had central organizations which looked after the activities of each community.

In Ashkenaz and Western Europe

Ashkenaz is the name of the Jewish communities of Germany, France, and Bohemia. Ashkenazi Jewry also includes the Jews who lived in Poland and Russia, most of whom emigrated from Germany. The most outstanding mark of Ashkenazi Jewry was Yiddish, a language derived from German in the Middle

used the word "Jew" as another word for merchant. During the First Crusade (the journey made by the Crusaders to Eretz Yisrael, to liberate Jerusalem from the Muslims) in 1096, bands of Crusaders destroyed many Jewish communities. Those worst hit were in the towns along the Rhine. The raiders demanded that the Jews convert, but the majority of Jews preferred to die for their faith.

Because the local rulers were not capable of defending the Jews, closer ties were created with the emperor of the "Holy Roman Empire," which included at that time the whole of central Europe. The emperor agreed to give better protection to the Jews, but they had to pay higher taxes to the imperial treasury in return. Now that they were thought of as property which could be used for profit, the Jews' position in society gradually weakened and their freedom of movement became restricted. Thus, as a result of the Crusades, the Jews had to leave trade, and they now worked mainly as money-changers or lenders.

The main activities of Ashkenazi sages centered around Jewish law—*Halakhah* in Hebrew. The word Halakhah comes from *halakh,* literally, to walk—along the path of righteousness. The outstanding figure in this field before the First Crusade was Rabbi Gershom, known as the "Light of the Diaspora" (960–1028). He headed the Yeshivah of Mainz and wrote both commentaries on the Talmud and answers to questions of Halakhah. His most famous regulation was the

ban on marrying more than one wife. The greatest Talmudic commentator was Rashi, Rabbi Solomon Bar Isaac (1040–1105). His commentary on the Talmud overshadowed all others prepared by Ashkenazi rabbis. Rashi's most famous work is his commentary on the Torah.

In the late 13th century, some half-million Jews, about half of the world's Jewish population, were living in Western Europe (including Ashkenaz). By around 1500, the Jewish population of this region was no more than 150,000. There were a number of reasons for this drop: riots, plagues, and—mainly—expulsions.

The first country to banish its Jews was England. Most of the Jews who had arrived in the British Isles in the 11th century made their living as moneylenders and in financial deals. While they loaned money to people from all walks of life, their main use was to supply funds to the king. For example, King Henry II (who reigned 1154–1189) owed the Jewish banker Aaron of Lincoln nearly £100,000, which was equal to a year's taxes to the royal treasury. During the 13th century, however, the kings demanded more and more money from the Jews, and their role of royal banker was gradually taken over by Christian money-dealers. Since they had stopped filling the role for which they had come to England, they were expelled.

The Jews were expelled from France for similar reasons. And so, between the end of the 13th century and the middle of the 16th, the Jews found themselves expelled from most of the countries of Western

This jug is from the 17th century. It was used for alcoholic drinks and is shaped in the figure of a Jewish tavern-keeper. It has phrases written on it mocking the Jewish leasing business.

The French king, in a painting from 1321, above left, is pointing at the Jews (marked with yellow circles), and is ordering them to leave.

Shown in the map: The Jews in Europe, from the 13th to the 15th centuries.

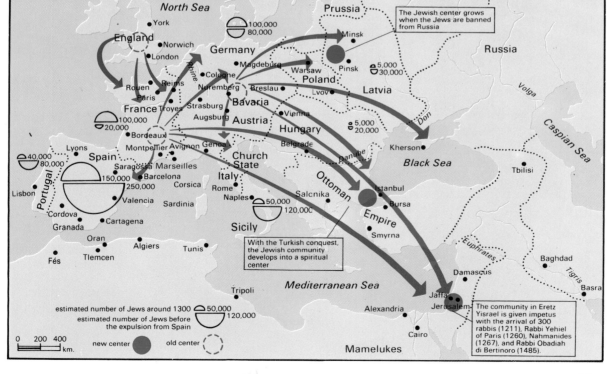

43

Europe, and were forced to seek new havens.

THE JEWISH COMMUNITY OF POLAND

The first Jews reached Poland during the Byzantine Empire, but by the Middle Ages most of the Jews in Poland were emigrants from Ashkenaz.

The Polish rulers from the 13th century on, seeking to develop their cities, welcomed Jews and other townspeople from Western Europe, particularly from Germany, and granted them a variety of privileges.

At first the major occupation of the Jews who came from Germany was that which they brought with them—moneylending. However, Poland offered them many new opportunities, and many Jews turned to business and trade.

In Poland, as in the countries of Western and Central Europe, the Catholic priests and the townspeople were responsible for the ill-feeling against the Jews. The Church, fearful of the Jewish influence, demanded that they be separated from the Christian population. The townspeople, fearing competition, fought to prevent Jewish businesses from growing, and tried to expel the Jews from the cities. Nevertheless, neither the king nor the higher nobility were willing to give up the benefits they were able to gain from the Jews.

As Poland expanded eastward during the 16th century, densely populated Jewish settlements sprang up in the Ukraine and Byelorussia. During the 16th and 17th centuries there were hundreds of Jewish communities in Poland. The communities governed themselves, and there were central organizations which looked after the interests of all the communities. One such central body was the Council of Four Lands—four areas where many Jews lived—which represented all of the Jews of Poland, and operated from the mid-16th century to 1764.

In the year 1648–1649 many Jewish communities were attacked and ravaged by Cossacks, led by Bogdan Chmielnicki. Russian and Swedish invasions followed. This struck a severe blow at the Jews of Poland. The prosperity and sense of security they had enjoyed was destroyed. The direction of Jewish immigration changed to Western Europe and, later, the United States.

9

FROM THE "GOLDEN AGE" TO THE EXPULSION FROM SPAIN

Before the Muslims conquered Spain in 711, the Jews were treated very harshly by the country's rulers, the Visigoths, and so they either fled or had to convert to Christianity. The Muslims, who needed useful, friendly people to help them look after the lands which they now ruled, gave the Jews special neighborhoods in many cities, and even trusted them to guard their fortresses. Both Jews and Christians paid heavy taxes to the new rulers, but the Muslims accepted people of other religions, and the Jews lived very well. In fact, the Jewish communities grew so large in the 10th and 12th centuries that the cities of Lucena, Granada, and Tarragona were known as "Jewish cities."

THE "GOLDEN AGE"

In the 11th and 12th centuries the Muslims and the Jews lived together in harmony. In this excellent atmosphere so many great works of poetry and philosophy were produced that this period is called by the Jews the "Golden Age." The culture of the "Golden Age" came about because of its special mixture of people and ideas. The Jews of Spain were in contact with the Jews of Babylonia and from them they learned the Talmud and the writings of the sages. But now the Spanish Jews created their own cultural center. Some Spanish Jews became important in the Muslim royal court. They served the monarchs as diplomats, physicians, financial advisors, and held other positions as well.

These courtiers were able to help Jewish poets, philosophers, writers, and scientists to produce works, both in Hebrew and Arabic. One of the first Jewish courtiers to become powerful was Hisdai ibn ("son of") Shaprut. He was an advisor to the Caliph (ruler) of Cordoba during the 10th century and was one of the Jews who made it possible for Jewish culture to flower.

Early in the 11th century, the region of Andalusia in the south of Spain was split into small rival states. In one of them lived the most famous Jewish courtier, Samuel ibn Nagrela (993–1056), who was also known as ha-Nagid (the leader, or nobleman). He was a poet, studied languages, and was well-versed in the Torah and Halakhah. For thirty years he served the kings of Granada as the commander of their army. Although devoted to the royal family he still dreamed of Zion and

Granada, shown at left, was the home of a flourishing Jewish community in the 11th century.

Hebrew literature rich in content and style was written in Spain under Muslim rule. The poem below by Joseph ibn Abitur (10th–11th century) deals with religious subjects.

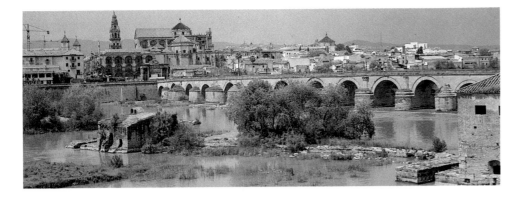

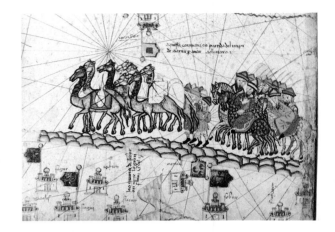

Shown above is the city of Cordoba, where Hisdai ibn Shaprut lived and worked.

A Hebrew inscription in the Cordoba synagogue (built 1314–1315), above right, links its construction to the eventual rebuilding of Jerusalem.

The map of the silk-trader's route to the Far East, shown on the right, was drawn by the Catalan Jew Abraham Cresques and his son Judah in the 14th century.

tried to protect his own people.

On the whole, the Jews of Spain lived peacefully and developed roots in the society around them. This gave them a character different from that of the other Jewish communities, especially those in Christian countries.

THE RECONQUEST AND THE JEWS

The Christians began to reconquer Spain in the 11th century, and by the end of the 13th century the country was almost completely back in their hands. At the same time, the Muslims became more suspicious of outsiders, and this made life harder and harder for the Jews. As for these later Christian kings, they used their Jewish subjects, as did the Muslims before them. The Jews knew the Muslim customs and various languages; they had ties with Jews in other parts of Spain and were not interested in coming to power themselves. All this, as well as the wealth and knowledge they had which could be used in settling and running the newly-conquered territories, made them very valuable to the Christian rulers. The kings granted the Jews a special status: their communities paid no taxes, they were given houses and lands, and they were allowed to rule themselves, although they still had to obey the local laws. Jewish communities grew in the Christian kingdoms in the north of the Iberian peninsula (the area covered by Spain and Portugal today): Castile-Leon, Aragon-Catalonia, Navarre, and Portugal.

Among the better-known Jews of this time was Judah Halevi, a physician and an important poet and philosopher who wrote both religious and secular literature. He was born in the town of Tudela in Muslim Spain (around 1075), and later moved to the Christian north. He hoped that the Jews would attain peace in the Christian countries but was disappointed. He decided to go to Eretz Yisrael. The story of his immigration is not clear. He travelled by sea to Egypt and, according to legend, he reached Jerusalem, where he was trampled to death by a horse.

Judah ibn Ezra, tax-collector for the Christian king Alfonso VII of Aragon (who ruled during the mid-12th century), was another outstanding Jew. He was in charge of an important Christian border fortress and helped the Jews who fled from the Muslim areas.

Rabbi Moses, son of Nahman (known as Ramban, or Nahmanides), also served a Spanish Christian king—James I. However, in 1263 the king forced him to take part in a religious debate with the Jewish

46

convert Pablo Christiani. The argument ended when Ramban was accused of slandering Christianity and was forced to flee Spain.

One of the outstanding Jewish philosophers of the 13th and early 14th centuries was Rabbi Moses, son of Maimon (abbreviated to Rambam, or Maimonides, 1138–1204). Maimonides was in favor of using allegory and reason to explain the holy texts, instead of accepting them exactly as they were written. He recorded these ideas in his books, *The Mishneh Torah* (Second Torah) and *The Guide of the Perplexed*. His approach upset some who feared that this would lead to alien beliefs. Nevertheless, his books are still considered to be of great importance.

At this time the *Kabbalah* (a mystical work, the study of hidden meanings) began to influence the intellectual world of Spanish Jewry. The largest part of the *Zohar* (brightness), the main book of the Kabbalah, is believed to have been written by Moses de Leon in the 13th century. According to popular tradition, however, the author was Shimon Bar Yohai, who lived more than 1,000 years earlier.

INQUISITION AND EXPULSION

Once the Christian victory over the Muslims was assured, the Jews were no longer needed. The Christian kings were more willing to accept the demands of the Catholic Church and the townspeople that the Jews be forced to convert. Some of the converts indeed became firm believers in their new religion. Many others, however, led a double life. Outwardly they lived as Christians, yet secretly they continued to observe some of the Jewish commandments. They called themselves *Anusim*, or forced ones. Documents from Spain and Portugal refer to these Jews as *Conversos* (converted ones), but the insulting

Above left is a synagogue in Toledo from the late 14th century. Later it was turned into a church.

The Toledo synagogue, shown at top, is from the 13th century, and is decorated in the Muslim style. It became the El Transito church.

An opening to a hide-away in a synagogue, above, recalling the way of life of the Anusim, the ancestors of the Jewish community of Rhode Island in the United States.

Left: Jewish communities in Spain in the 13th and 14th centuries.

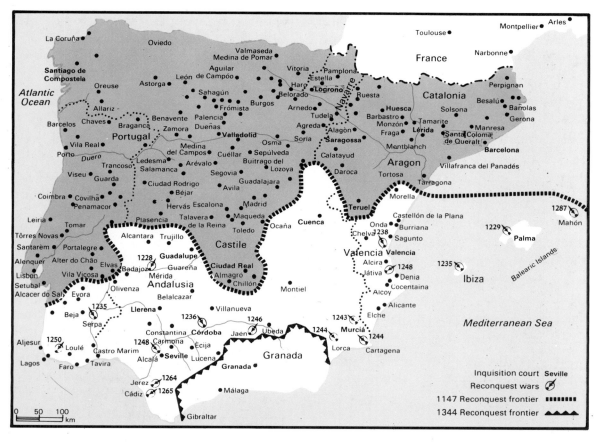

Inquisition court	Seville
Reconquest wars	
1147 Reconquest frontier	
1344 Reconquest frontier	

change their ways were given a variety of punishments: self-torture, fasting, prayer, pilgrimages to holy sites, and even public whippings or imprisonment. Prisoners who refused to change their beliefs were burned at the stake in a public ceremony.

On March 31, 1492—shortly after Granada, the last Muslim stronghold in Spain, was conquered by the Christians—the King and Queen of Spain ordered all of the Jews to convert within three months, or leave the country. Hundreds of thousands of Jews left Spain for

The punishment of burning at the stake, seen here in Berruqueta's painting, was the final judgment of the Inquisition against outward converts.

Above right: The tombstone of King Ferdinand and Queen Isabella. They signed the expulsion decree at about the time that Columbus set sail for America.

name most people called them was *Marranos* (pigs). Spanish society remained hostile toward the Conversos. Now that they were free of the anti-Jewish laws, Christian Spaniards openly feared competition from the Jews. Prejudice against them was voiced in the sermons of priests and in various writings, and eventually in riots which led to actual warfare between the Christians and the "New Christians."

Anusim who had been reported observing Jewish practices were brought before the Inquisition—the Roman Catholic court that tried non-believers—and questioned under terrible torture. Those who confessed their sins and promised to

other European countries, mainly to the Ottoman Empire. The Christians' victory over the Muslims had meant the end of the Jewish community of Spain.

After the expulsion, only Anusim remained in Spain and Portugal. Since their Jewishness had not been rooted out, they were persecuted by the Inquisition and this led to many Anusim leaving. In the eastern Muslim countries, they were received into communities already established by Jews expelled from Spain. In Christian Western Europe and on the American continent, they tried to set up new communities in which they could live once more as Jews.

10
IN THE SHADOW OF THE CRESCENT

In the 14th century there was a small state in northwest Anatolia in Turkey ruled by a prince called an emir. The people who lived there were Muslims, whose symbol is the crescent. The emir started a "holy war" against his neighbor, the Christian Byzantine Empire. In 1453 the Turks captured Constantinople, the Byzantine capital, and this was the end of the Byzantine Empire. The new Turkish empire now began to grow very quickly. It was called the Ottoman Empire after Emir Othman I. By the end of the 16th century, the Ottoman Empire ruled the Balkan countries (Turkey, Greece, and their neighbors), Southern Russia, and the Middle East, including Eretz Yisrael and the southern coast of the Mediterranean Sea. The great enemy of the Ottoman Empire was the "Holy Roman Empire" of Christian Europe in the west.

Jews lived in many of the countries ruled by the Ottoman Empire. Some had been there from the time of the Romans. Many thousands more came to these countries after they were expelled from Spain and Portugal. The Ottoman rulers were glad to have the Jews settle in their countries. The Jews had a lot of experience in finance, trade, and administration, and they could help the Ottoman Empire grow stronger. So in the 15th and 16th centuries, there were many Jews living under Muslim rule, both in the Ottoman Empire and in other Muslim countries such as Morocco, Persia, Afghanistan, and Yemen.

PROTECTED SUBJECTS

Most of the Jews lived in separate neighborhoods in the large cities along the Mediterranean coast. The Jewish quarters in the Muslim cities were called *mellahs*.

There were also other Jewish

A street in a Jewish neighborhood in Fez, in Morocco. The house on the left was the home of Maimonides. He probably lived here in the years 1160–1165. The 13 water clocks symbolize the 13 Principles of Faith he defined.

Exiles from Spain and Portugal (1492–1497) moved to other countries, as shown in the map.

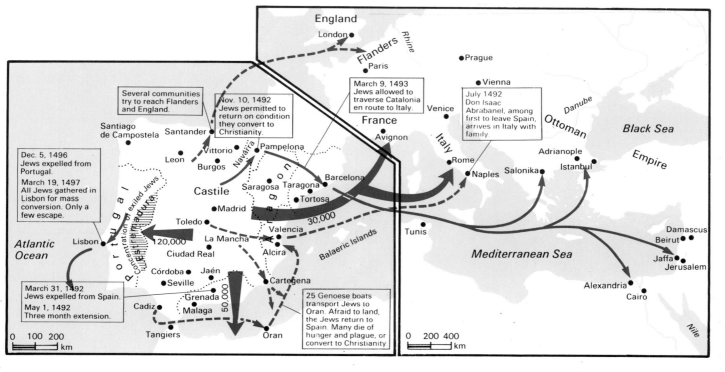

but it also showed everyone that they were "non-believers." The Jews also had to pay other taxes to the local rulers. In order to show that the Jews were different and were not as good as Muslims, there

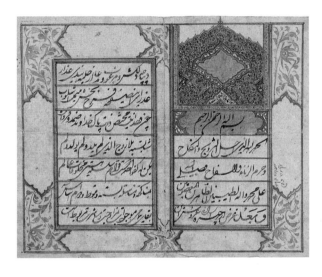

A book of religious readings for holidays from Kurdistan (1864), above at top.

Skullcaps, above top right, embroidered in the style of Afghanistan (left) and Georgia, Russia (right).

Two marriage contracts from Meshed, are shown above. Although they look similar, the one on the left is a Jewish contract from 1901, written in Hebrew; the one on the right is a Muslim contract from 1902, written in Persian.

communities farther away, in cities along important trade routes, where people brought Chinese silk and Asian carpets and coffee to be sold to European merchants.

The Muslims treated the non-Muslim people in their countries according to the laws of their religion—Islam. They divided everyone into "believers" (meaning Muslims) or "non-believers." The Jews and Christians were called "The People of the Book" because their religions are based on the Bible. Because of this they were given protection and religious, social, and legal freedom, and the Muslims did not try to convert them to Islam. However, they had to pay a special tax. This meant that the government would protect them,

were many things that they were not allowed to do. They could not say their prayers out loud, they could not build any new synagogues, they had to wear special clothes, they could not own land, they could not have servants, they could not build their houses higher than Muslim houses, and they could not even ride horses.

The Jews were trusted by the Ottomans, so they were usually treated better than the Christians. However, sometimes local rulers made life hard for the Jews by forcing them to pay high taxes or forbidding them to do many things.

This situation became worse toward the end of the 16th century. In many places the Jews were not left to live in peace. Lies were told about the Jews, and the Muslims tried to make them convert to Islam. This happened mainly in countries ruled by the Shi'ites, a group of Muslims who were extremely religious. For example, in 1679 all of the Jews who lived in the city of San'a in Yemen left their homes and went to live in Mawza, because the Muslims of San'a wanted them to convert to Islam. In 1839 in Meshed, Persia, the Jews were robbed and murdered. The few Jews who were still alive were forced to convert to Islam against their will. The forced converts of Meshed were called the "New Muslims." In public they were Muslims, but secretly they lived as Jews. And in 1840 in Damascus, Syria, the Jews were falsely accused of murdering a monk and his Muslim servant in order to use their blood in a Passover ritual.

GREAT OPPORTUNITIES

The Ottomans let the Jews earn their living in any way they wanted to. Many Jews worked in occupations concerning food, so that they would be sure they had the kind of food required by the laws of Judaism. Some Jews worked for the Ottoman rulers and army. They supplied them with everything they needed, from loans of money to food and clothing. Other Jews were goldsmiths and jewelry-makers.

Large numbers of Jews lived in port cities, mainly in Constantinople (which the Jews called Kushta), Salonika, and Izmir. In these places they worked in very different professions. They were porters, laborers, and sailors. In Salonika, for example, which was a very important city because its port was used by all the Balkan countries, most of the port workers in the 19th and 20th centuries were Jews. Because of this the port was closed on the Sabbath and the Jewish holy days. But most of the Jews worked in small businesses and international trade. They were very successful traders because they knew European languages (after all, they often had to move from place to place) and they had relatives in different countries.

Some Jews were even important in the government. They were the rulers' doctors, diplomats, and advisers. One of the most famous of these was Don Joseph Nasi, who lived in the 16th century. The Ottoman emperor, called the Sultan, listened very carefully to the advice he got from him. It was Don Joseph who gave him the idea to conquer Cyprus, which was then ruled by Venice. Don Joseph had a lot of power and knew many important

Above is a Syrian wine jug from the 18th century.

Jewelry-making was a Jewish occupation in all Muslim countries. Below left are silver Torah ornaments from Persia, and jewelry from Bukhara.

Below center: A Jewish woman in front of the port of Constantinople. The engraving was made around 1650.

The men in the photograph below were porters in the port of Salonika.

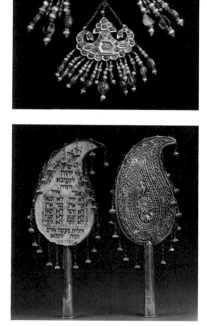

51

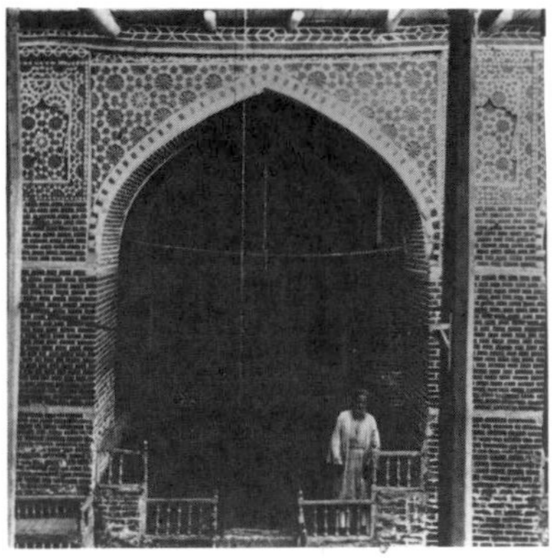

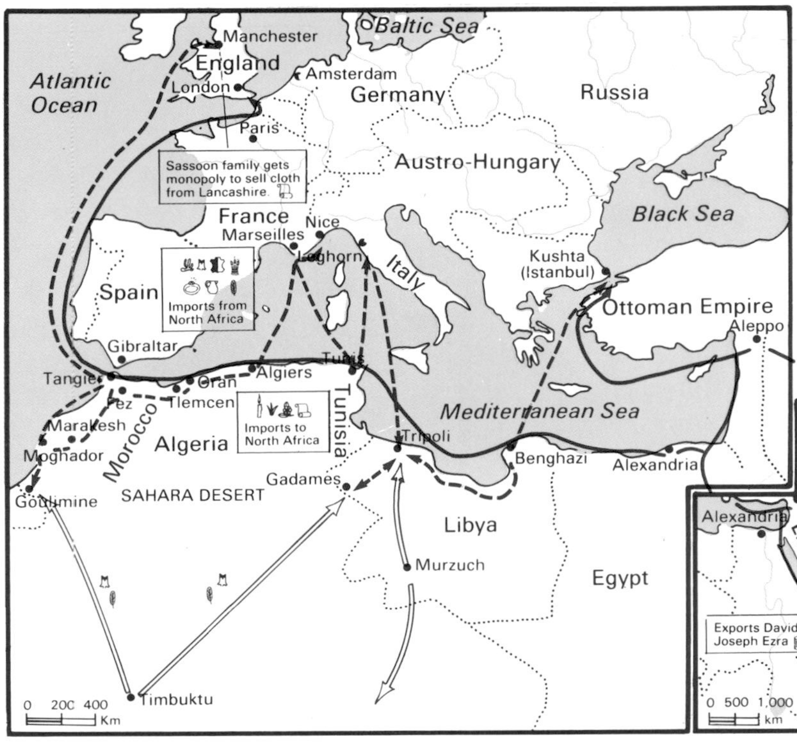

Manchester
Baltic Sea
England
Amsterdam
London
Atlantic Ocean
Germany
Russia
Paris
Sassoon family gets monopoly to sell cloth from Lancashire
Austro-Hungary
France
Marseilles
Nice
Black Sea
Leghorn
Italy
Kushta (Istanbul)
Spain
Imports from North Africa
Ottoman Empire
Aleppo
Gibraltar
Tunis
Tangier
Oran
Algiers
Fez
Tlemcen
Tunisia
Marakesh
Morocco
Algeria
Imports to North Africa
Mediterranean Sea
Mogador
Tripoli
Benghazi
Alexandria
Goulimine
SAHARA DESERT
Gadames
Libya
Murzuch
Egypt
Timbuktu
0 200 400 Km

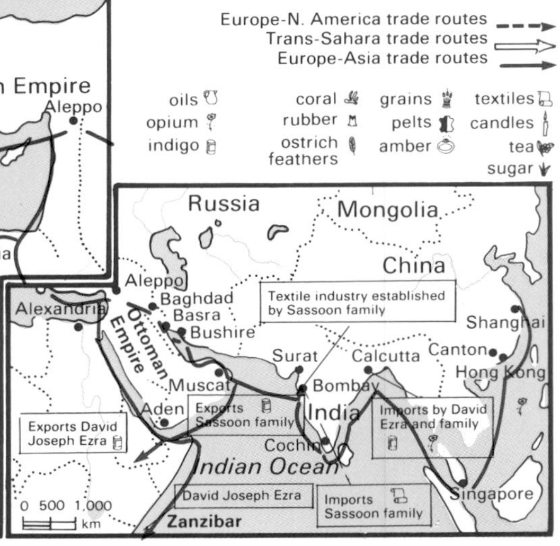

Europe-N. America trade routes
Trans-Sahara trade routes
Europe-Asia trade routes
oils
opium
indigo
coral
rubber
ostrich feathers
grains
pelts
amber
textiles
candles
tea
sugar
Russia
Mongolia
China
Aleppo
Alexandria
Baghdad
Basra
Bushire
Ottoman Empire
Textile industry established by Sassoon family
Shanghai
Canton
Hong Kong
Surat
Calcutta
Muscat
Bombay
Aden
Exports Sassoon family
India
Imports by David Ezra and family
Exports David Joseph Ezra
Cochin
Indian Ocean
David Joseph Ezra
Imports Sassoon family
Singapore
0 500 1,000 km
Zanzibar

The ancient synagogue in Baghdad, far right, was rebuilt several times in the 17th and 19th centuries.

Trade routes in Europe, Africa, the Middle East, and the Far East in the second half of the 19th centuries are shown on these maps.

In Yemen schooling took place in a Khutab—a class like the one shown below right.

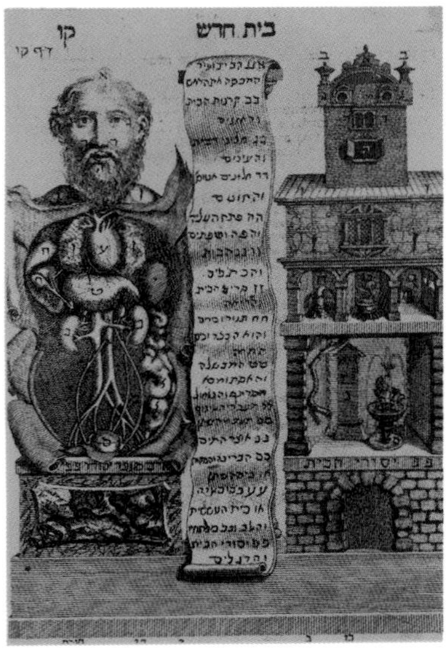

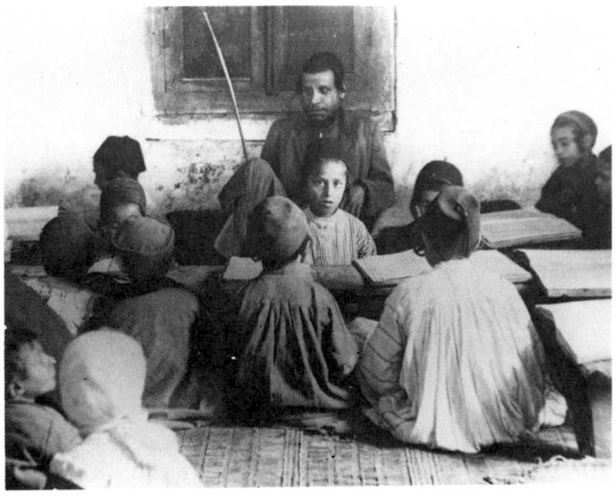

A page from a medical book, shown above, compares the human body to a house. The book was written by Tuvia, son of Moshe Hacohen, who was the Sultan's doctor at the end of the 17th century.

people, so he was able to help his fellow Jews.

Emissaries from Eretz Yisrael visited the Jewish communities in the Ottoman Empire. They came to collect money to help the Jews in their homeland. By moving from place to place, these emissaries strengthened the ties among these many communities, and also between the Jewish communities in the Diaspora and the Jews in Eretz Yisrael. They also spread news of important religious decisions throughout the Ottoman Empire, so that even Jews who lived far away from others behaved very much in the same way.

In the middle of the 19th century, the status of the Jews in Muslim countries improved. The Sultan cancelled the special poll tax and introduced a new method of collecting taxes—according to the value of the property. The Jews were then given the same legal and civil rights as all the other people in the Empire.

After World War I (1914–1918) most of the Jews in Muslim countries moved away. Some went to Western Europe, the United States, or Latin America. Most of them went to the Land of Israel. There were several reasons that made them decide to leave. Firstly, the Ottoman Empire was broken up after the war. The Arabs now wanted to rule their own countries, and they did not like the Jews at all. Secondly, the Zionist movement, which wanted to bring all the Jews to the Land of Israel, became stronger. And finally, in 1948 the State of Israel was established. Today, very few Jews live in Muslim countries.

11
IS THE MESSIAH COMING?

Jews believe that one day the Messiah will come, to prepare the world for the time when God will rule over it. The Messiah is mentioned in the Bible, and in many other Jewish books. All of them speak of a miracle which will bring about the rule of God, and then everyone in the world will live in complete happiness and peace.

Throughout history there have been groups of people who thought they knew exactly when the Messiah would come or just who he was. There were even people who said that they themselves were the Messiah, but of course they weren't. We call them "false messiahs." This usually happened when life was particularly hard for the Jews, because it is believed that the Jews

will suffer very much just before the Messiah comes, like a mother who suffers a lot of pain in order to give birth to a wonderful child.

MESSIANIC MOVEMENTS IN DIFFERENT COUNTRIES
The first group of people who expected the imminent arrival of the Messiah lived in Eretz Yisrael during the time of the Second Temple. They believed that God would send the Messiah to save them from the

cruel rule of the Romans. There were other "false messiahs" in the Eastern countries in the 8th century, during the First Crusade (1096–1099) in Byzantium, during the Spanish Inquisition, and at other difficult times in Jewish history. For example, for about ten years, from 1523 to 1532, David Reuveni and Solomon Molcho convinced many Jews in Europe, Egypt, and Eretz Yisrael that the Messiah was coming very soon. Reuveni said that he was a general of the army of the Ten Tribes—the lost people of the Kingdom of Israel who are supposed to appear again when the Messiah comes. He brought the Pope a plan to conquer Jerusalem from the Ottomans. The Pope sent him to the King of Portugal. In the Portuguese court he met the king's scribe, Solomon Molcho. The two men then

Tradition says that when the Messiah comes, the dead will be brought back to life and the bodies of the most holy people will roll to the Mount of Olives in Jerusalem. This picture of a tree on the Mount of Olives illustrates a verse from the Book of the Prophet Zechariah in the Bible. It is from Saragossa, Spain, in 1404.

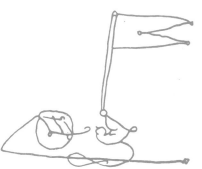

This is how Solomon Molcho signed his name.

The Prophet Ezekiel, in his vision of the dry bones, described how the dead would be brought back to life. The picture of his vision, on the left, is shown in a 3rd-century fresco (wall painting) in the Dura Europos Synagogue on the Euphrates River.

very strangely. He claimed that he was the Messiah, but the rabbis of Izmir did not believe him and they sent him away from the city. In 1662 he came to Jerusalem. A year later he went to Egypt to collect money for the Jews in Jerusalem. In Egypt he married a woman named Sarah, who had escaped from Poland where the

The Messiah at the gates of Jerusalem on a donkey, above (from a Passover Haggadah produced in Italy in 1478). The Haggadah tells the story of how the Jews were saved from slavery in Egypt, so it has become a symbol of how the Jews will be saved from suffering when the Messiah comes.

The Synagogue of Ha-Ari (Luria) in Safed is shown in the photograph on the right.

A prayerbook from Morocco (1791) is shown in the center. It includes prayers written by Luria to "repair" the world.

His regal splendor was one of the things that made Shabbetai Zevi so popular. He was handsome and had a beautiful voice—and a wild temper. The picture of Shabbetai Zevi riding a horse is from Germany, 1666.

went to Charles V, who was the emperor of the "Holy Roman Empire," which controlled large parts of Europe. They wanted the Emperor to support their plan, but he sentenced Molcho to death and threw Reuveni into prison.

When the Messiah comes, all of the Jews are supposed to be in Eretz Yisrael. So a lot of people went to Eretz Yisrael in the 16th century. They wanted to be ready for the Messiah. A group of them gathered in the city of Safed. Some were Kabbalists who believed in secret and mysterious interpretations of the Bible. They were deeply religious and lived a very simple life.

The two most famous Kabbalists in Safed were Rabbi Moses Cordovero (1522–1570) and his student Rabbi Isaac Luria Ashkenazi, known as Ha-Ari—"the Lion." "The Lion" believed that flaws were made in the Creation, and it was the mission of the Jewish people all over the world to "repair" these mistakes. They could do it through good intentions and certain actions, like prayer and fasting. When the "repairs" had been made, the Messiah would come. Luria had a very great influence on many Jews throughout the world. Many people believed that by doing what he suggested, they could help make that day come sooner.

SHABBETAI ZEVI

Shabbetai Zevi was the most famous of the false Messiahs. He was born in Izmir in Turkey in 1626. He was a very odd person and often behaved

Sabethai Sevi, der Falsche Messias.

come. They fasted, donated money, and began to prepare for the journey to Eretz Yisrael. There were stories of signs and miracles, and rumors that the Ten Lost Tribes had been seen in Africa, in Mecca, or near Gaza. People became more and more excited.

Jews of all kinds believed in Shabbetai Zevi, from the religious leaders to the simple people. He had many followers in all of the Jewish communities both in the east and west—from Yemen and North Africa to Poland, Holland, and England. There were not many Jews in these countries who did not believe that Shabbetai Zevi was the Messiah.

Shabbetai Zevi's popularity frightened the Turkish government. In September 1666, he was arrested and given a choice—either convert to Islam or die. He decided to convert, and told his followers to do the same thing. In August 1672, Shabbetai Zevi was arrested again. This time he was accused of not being a good Muslim and of breaking the law, and he was sent to prison. Four years later, Shabbetai Zevi—the Messiah who had changed his religion—died.

Cossacks attacked the Jews and killed many of them. On his way back to Jerusalem, he stopped in Gaza to speak with Rabbi Nathan, a young "soul healer." Nathan had a vision in which he saw that Shabbetai Zevi was really the Messiah. He excitedly announced this to the public and many people believed him.

Nathan of Gaza wrote letters to the Jewish communities outside of Eretz Yisrael and told them about Shabbetai Zevi. At that time the Jews in many countries were being treated very cruelly and even murdered, so they were glad to believe that the Messiah had really

Nathan of Gaza, Shabbetai Zevi's prophet, shown at top left.

The Temple and Jerusalem have a special place in Jewish tradition, especially concerning the coming of the Messiah. At the end of time, Jerusalem will be rebuilt and will stand forever as a spiritual center. The picture on the left is from the Hamburg Haggadah, 1768.

"Shabbetai Zevi, the False Messiah" is written on the 18th-century copper engraving, above, from Germany.

12

FREEDOM AND EQUALITY—FOR JEWS AS WELL

In the 18th century, a movement arose in western Europe demanding equal rights, security, and freedom for all people. This movement was started by the middle class or townspeople—the "bourgeoisie" (*bourg* means town) who formed the "enlightenment movement." The bourgeoisie was a new class of people, which arose because of the industrial revolution. They were against the division of society into the aristocracy and the clergy, who had rights, and the majority of the people, who had none. This new enlightenment movement was based upon the belief that all people should be judged according to their worth and intelligence, that is, according to reason, and not according to feeling or religious belief. It argued that all people should be equal before the law. This new spirit resulted in the American Declaration of Independence in 1776, and in the Declaration of the

The Jewish peddler was seen by enlightened Jews as a figure who needed "improving."

Rights of Man of the French Revolution in 1789. Thus, equal rights for all citizens became the law in the western European countries and in America.

EQUAL RIGHTS FOR THE JEWS
How did this new idea sweeping across Europe affect the Jews? During the 17th and 18th centuries, Jews in western and central Europe enjoyed a protected status. When Jews had requested to settle in a certain place, the ruler of the country or of the town decided on how long they could stay according to how much money his treasury would gain from them. Although protected, the Jews did not enjoy regular civil rights. Their freedom of movement was limited and they were not allowed to hold certain occupations. While the Jewish communities did have self-rule, or autonomy, the non-Jewish rulers often interfered in their affairs, and the threat of expulsion constantly hung over their heads. By the end of the 18th century, conditions improved, and Jews were gradually allowed to hold a greater variety of occupations, but their status under the law did not change.

Beginning in the 1780s, people started arguing over whether the Jews should become citizens. Many felt that the Jews first had to be "reformed" and "made useful," while others thought that they would "improve" as a result of equality. Nobody questioned the fact that the Jews "ought" to be "improved." The Christians accused the Jews of working in such "unproductive" professions as

peddling and moneylending. Because they linked these professions with greed and dishonesty, they believed the Jews to be greedy and dishonest as well. The opinion that the Jews were "unproductive" even influenced some Jews, particularly the enlightened intellectuals. They found European culture and ideas exciting and their Jewish world no longer satisfied them. So they, too, accepted the idea that they should "reform." The Jewish emancipation movement, which fought for equal rights, urged the Jews to improve themselves in order to gain equality. The large population of poor Jews were urged to move to more productive professions such as the skilled trades and agriculture. During the 19th century, many Jews indeed held a wider range of occupations, and many changed their way of living and dressed in the style of the non-Jews around them.

The Jewish intellectuals rejected the Yiddish language, which set the Jews apart from their neighbors. Through their schools and the articles they published, they encouraged Jews to learn the national tongue, and the Bible was translated for them into German. On the other hand, biblical Hebrew, a language which was highly regarded by Christians, was also taught. By the middle of the 19th century, Yiddish was no longer the most widely spoken language of Jews in central and western Europe.

The biggest issue was Judaism itself—a religion whose rituals kept the Jews apart from their non-Jewish neighbors. The enlightened intellectual wanted to be a Jew as well as a regular citizen of a European country. A few despaired of finding a solution and converted to Christianity. Others moved away from a traditional Jewish way of life, hoping to become part of the society, but they were not willing to give up their Jewish identity completely. They felt they should observe the basic moral laws of Judaism, especially the Ten Commandments and the teachings of the Prophets. Their motto was a Talmudic saying, that "the Almighty had shown great charity in scattering the Jewish People among the nations" so that they might spread the lofty and universal moral principles of Judaism. This was how the emancipated "German" or "French" Jew came to be.

Cover of the book The Alsatian Jews—Should They Be Granted Equal Rights? *(1790) shown above left. It urged the Jews to take up skilled trades and agriculture.*

Shown in the painting above, the Nathanson family from Copenhagen, wearing their best non-Jewish style festive clothes.

The Book of Psalms above, translated into German by Moses Mendelssohn.

57

EMANCIPATION HARD TO GAIN

Revolutionary France was the first country in Europe to give equal rights to the Jews, on the 27th of September, 1791. In the French parliament, those who were against

Heinrich Heine (1797–1856), right, a German-Jewish poet and writer, converted to Christianity at the age of 28.

Napoleon is seen in the 1802 engraving, far right, granting freedom of worship to members of different religions.

The synagogue in Strasbourg, far right, was designed by the Jewish architect Ludwig Levy. Outwardly the building, built in 1898 and destroyed by the Nazis, looks like a church.

The time it took to grant the Jews emancipation differed from place to place, as shown in the map. In some countries emancipation was achieved by passing a law, in others it happened gradually. In certain countries no rights at all were granted during the 19th century.

giving the Jews equal rights argued that the Jews were loyal to another country (Eretz Yisrael) and to another king (Almighty God). They also spoke against the way the Jewish religion kept itself apart, and described the Jews' so-called "bad" characteristics. Some devout Christians even said that the Jews had to continue living separately so they might fulfill the destiny that Providence had thrust upon them. Those in favor of equality replied that Jews, as human beings, were entitled to the "natural right" of joining French society on condition that they truly wished to do so and stopped keeping themselves apart as a nation. "To the Jews as a nation nothing shall be granted; to the Jews

as human beings—everything," was the argument of one French statesman. Equality was given to the Jews as individuals, but they were expected to abandon all their traditional customs and institutions. Many Jews found it very hard to give up these things.

Emancipation spread during the 19th century, mainly as a result of the conquests made by France during the Revolution and under Napoleon. Nevertheless, even though equal rights were given to the Jews in most of the countries of Europe, only a small change was made in the negative feelings about them, and propaganda against them continued. The gap between the Jews' expectations and reality widened.

13

IN THE EMBRACE OF POLAND AND RUSSIA

In the mid-17th century, many Jews in Poland lost their homes, and even their lives, in attacks by Cossacks who were military guards on the border of Russia and Poland. Those who had believed in the false Messiah Shabbetai Zevi now realized their mistake. In the middle of the 18th century, a new movement called Hasidism (from the Hebrew word *Hasid* for a God-fearing person) suggested a way of making the Messiah come sooner. It offered hope to these people and it quickly became very popular.

THE SPREAD OF HASIDISM

The founder of Hasidism was Rabbi Israel, son of Eliezer—the Ba'al Shem Tov or The Besht (1700–1760). *Ba'al Shem* means "miracle worker" and *Tov* means "good" in Hebrew. Rabbi Israel was born in the Polish province of Podolia, where the Cossacks had attacked many towns. He earned his living digging clay in the Carpathian Mountains, and there he learned about medicinal herbs. In his thirties, he began to travel from place to place as a miracle worker who could cure diseases of the body and the soul, not only with his herbs, but also with vows, charms, and

prayer. He was a famous storyteller, and all sorts of people came to him for advice and guidance. A group of these people became his followers, called Hasidim. His way of life strongly influenced them. They were particularly impressed by the way he prayed. He prayed so intensely that he would faint. When he fainted he had visions. He saw his own soul rising to heaven where he asked the Messiah and the angels to help the Jewish people. The Ba'al Shem Tov was the first Hasidic leader, called a *zaddik* (righteous man).

After the death of the Ba'al Shem Tov, his follower, Rabbi Dov Baer of Mezhirech (1704–1773) became the leader of Hasidism. Many people came to Mezhirech from different parts of Poland to ask his advice, and when they went home they spread the ideas of the Hasidic movement.

Hasidim deeply believe in the importance of devoutness in prayer, of serving God in joy while dealing with the matters of everyday life, and of happiness and absolute belief in the zaddik. Unique qualities enable the zaddik, according to the Hasidim, to come closer to God than ordinary people, and thus qualify

A hasid and his wife in typical clothes.

Rabbi Shneur Zalman of Lyady, below, founded Habad Hasidism.

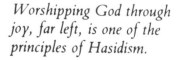

Worshipping God through joy, far left, is one of the principles of Hasidism.

Two views of a ritual wine cup from 18th- or 19th-century Poland, made of melted silver coins given by the zaddik to his followers for luck.

59

Pale of Settlement ───
Regional Border ───
Provincial Border ⋯⋯⋯
Jewish population in region 724.500
percent of Jews in province (13.6%)
Jewish population in province 345.000

more than 40,000 Jews ⊡
30-40,000 Jews ◉
20-30,000 Jews •
10-20,000 Jews ○
city barred to Jews (by order of Nicholas I) ▲

Above: The Pale of Settlement.

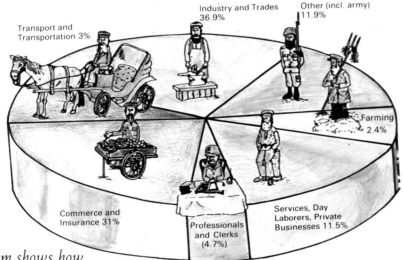

This diagram shows how Russian Jews earned their living in the 19th century.

The Gaon Rabbi Elijah of Vilna, top right, was the greatest opponent of Hasidism.

A Jewish knife-sharpener, above right, went from place to place with his tools.

him to act as mediator between God and the believer.

The movement attracted religious scholars, and also many simple Jews who had to work to earn a living and did not have much time to study. Hasidism spread from Podolia to Western Poland and Eastern Russia, and soon had tens of thousands of followers.

A group of Hasidim followed Rabbi Shneur Zalman of Lyady and founded Habad Hasidism. The name "Habad" comes from the first letters of the Hebrew words for wisdom, understanding, and knowledge. Habad Hasidim believe that observing the commandments and logical thinking are the way to God.

There were also large groups of Jews who opposed Hasidism. They were called *Mitnaggedim* ("opposers" in Hebrew). They thought that the noisy prayers and enthusiastic movements of the Hasidim showed that they were undignified and rowdy. Over the years, the Hasidim and the Mitnaggedim existed side by side in Jewish communities.

THE PALE OF SETTLEMENT

At the time that the Hasidic movement was growing, Poland was conquered and divided up by its neighbors Prussia, Austria, and Russia. Now many Jews lived under Russian rule, including those who lived in regions that had been conquered from the Ottoman Empire. During the 19th century, there were about five million Jews in Russia. In fact, in 1880, almost two-thirds of all the Jews in the world lived there.

The Jews in Russia were only allowed to live in a region called the Pale of Settlement. It was quite a large area in which about 11% of the population were Jews. In many small towns, most of the people were Jews. There were very few occupations that the Jews were allowed to practice. Most of them provided services for the non-Jewish population. It was very difficult to make a living, and the government made it harder by demanding heavy taxes, so the people in the Pale of Settlement were very poor.

The tsars (the Russian kings) saw the Jews as foreigners who hurt the economy of Russia. They wanted the Jews to "reform"—to change their

way of life and become part of Russian society. Some of the tsars tried to force the Jews to do this, and other tsars wanted to give them special rights to encourage them to "reform." Alexander I, who was the Tsar from 1801 to 1825, tried both methods. On the other hand, Tsar Nicholas I (1825–1855) was very cruel to the Jews. He even made a law that required the Jewish communities to supply a certain number of boys aged twelve for military training. Alexander II (1855–1881) was more liberal. He changed or cancelled some of the harsher laws. He also allowed some of the Jews, like the wealthy merchants, academics, skilled workers, and former soldiers, to live outside the Pale of Settlement, and they established large communities in St. Petersburg and Moscow.

On the whole, the Russian tsars did not succeed in "reforming" the Jews. Most educated Jews in Russia believed that the Jews could have a broad general education and still keep their Jewish way of life. The Jewish movement called *Haskalah*

This is a poor courtyard in the Jewish section of Kazimierz in Poland. It was painted by Alexander Kutzich (1830–1877).

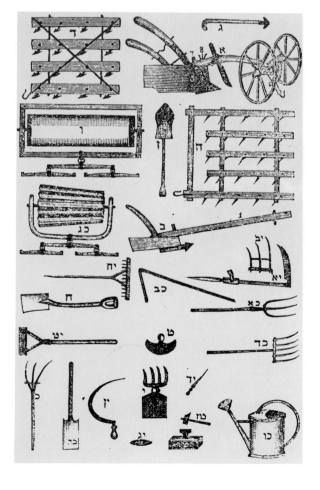

(which means "education" or "knowledge" in Hebrew) produced many Russian authors and poets who wrote in Yiddish and Hebrew. Some of them are considered the fathers of modern Hebrew literature.

A page from Guide to Farming, *left, a book written by H. S. Schneider in the 19th century, which reflected the Jews' desire to be farmers.*

After the Pogrom, *right, was painted by Maurice Minkowsky (1881–1930), a Jewish artist from Warsaw.*

Scrolls of the Torah were buried after they were torn and thrown to the ground in the pogrom at Kishinev, far right.

stronger, and the government was afraid of them. Since many of the socialist leaders were Jews, the government said that these parties were working for the Jews and not for the good of the Russian people. So again the Jews were attacked in a second wave of pogroms between 1903 and 1906.

The first of these pogroms took

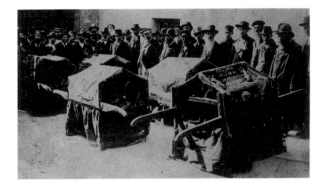

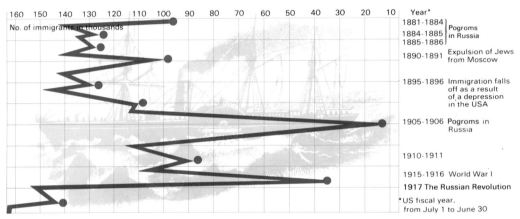

No. of immigrants in thousands																Year*	
160	150	140	130	120	110	100	90	80	70	60	50	40	30	20	10	1881-1884	Pogroms in Russia

1881-1884
1884-1885 Pogroms in Russia
1885-1886

1890-1891 Expulsion of Jews from Moscow

1895-1896 Immigration falls off as a result of a depression in the USA

1905-1906 Pogroms in Russia

1910-1911

1915-1916 World War I

1917 The Russian Revolution

*US fiscal year, from July 1 to June 30

The number of Jews entering the U.S. after each of the pogroms in Russia is shown in the above diagram.

The painting on the right shows Jews leaving Russia after the pogroms of 1881, on a ship sailing for America.

THE JEWS LEAVE RUSSIA

Until 1881, the Jews lived in relative security in Russia. In that year the pogroms—attacks on Jewish quarters—began. When Tsar Alexander II was killed in 1881, the first wave of pogroms (1881–1884) started. One of the people who was sentenced to death for killing the Tsar was a Jewish woman, Hassia Helfman. The motive for the attacks probably came from the people close to Tsar Alexander III (the murdered tsar's son). They were happy when people were angry with the Jews instead of with the government.

The first reaction of many Jews was to leave Russia. Other Jews joined the socialists, who wanted to change the government of Russia. The socialist parties became even

place in Kishinev during Passover of 1903. The Jews were shocked by the number of people who were killed and also by the fact that they were helpless to protect themselves. Many Jewish youngsters formed self-defense societies. Their only weapons were axes, sticks and stones. And when pogroms broke out in Gomel soon after those in Kishinev, these youngsters stopped the rioters and defended their communities.

Mainly because of the pogroms and the terror during World War I and the Russian Revolution, about two and a half million Jews left Russia between 1881 and 1920. Most of them went to the United States. Some went to other parts of Europe or to Eretz Yisrael.

14

THE AWAKENING OF JEWISH NATIONALISM

Since the first exile from the Land of Israel, the Jewish people prayed daily to return to their homeland. During the first half of the 19th century, many European nations became independent. The Jews, too, desired an independent nation of their own. Being equal citizens in European countries was not enough. More and more Jews wanted to return to the "land of our fathers."

FORERUNNERS OF ZIONISM

Both religious and non-religious Jews were among the first to herald the call to leave Europe and settle in Eretz Yisrael. Two notable rabbis, Zvi Hirsch Kalischer, who was born in Poland, and Judah Alkalai, who was born in Serbia, believed that if the Jews went to Eretz Yisrael, the Messiah would come sooner. Moses Hess, a philosopher and one of the founders of German socialism, wanted to establish a free Jewish society in Eretz Yisrael. These three men not only wrote and preached their ideas,

settled in Eretz Yisrael in 1871.

In 1881 there were pogroms in Russia—attacks on Jewish towns and villages in which many people were killed. Now more and more Jews began to realize that the Jews needed a country of their own where they would be safe. Many societies of Hovevei Zion or Hibat Zion, Lovers of Zion (the Biblical name for the Land of Israel), were founded throughout Russia. Their members believed that immigration to Eretz Yisrael was the only solution to the problem of the Jews.

One of these groups was called Bilu. The name Bilu comes from the first letters of the Hebrew words of the Biblical verse: "House of Jacob, come ye and let us go." Their aim was "the political-economic and national-spiritual revival of the Jewish people in Eretz Yisrael."

In 1882, Leon Pinsker, a physician from Russia, wrote a pamphlet called "Auto-emancipation," and it was published in Berlin. Pinsker considered anti-Semitism—hatred of

The cover of the bylaws of the Bilu Society, above.

Lower left: Examples of Jewish journals published in the 19th century. Their main topic was Zionism.

The picture of Jerusalem, below, was painted by Samuel Schulman and given to the philanthropist Benjamin de Rothschild. Schulman sent paintings like this to Jewish philanthropists in order to encourage them to support the Zionist idea. Beside each musical instrument is a verse from the Bible which describes it.

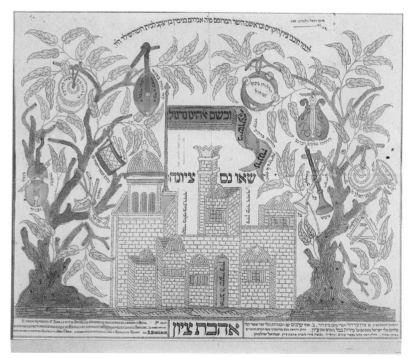

but they also organized groups of people who were prepared to settle in the homeland, and they tried to persuade wealthy Jews to buy land in Eretz Yisrael. Alkalai actually

Above: Petach Tikva, one of the first new Jewish settlements in Eretz Yisrael founded by the members of Hovevei Zion. The name comes from the Bible and means "door of hope."

Above right is a membership card for the First Zionist Congress, with a decorative border of sayings about Zion.

Alfred Dreyfus was publicly humiliated after his trial, above left. His army stripes were torn off and his sword was broken.

Herzl in Turkey, above center.

Nahum Sokolow, shown above right, covered the First Zionist Congress as a journalist. Here he is seen during a visit to Jerusalem.

the Jews—an incurable disease, and Zionism— immigration to Eretz Yisrael—the only medicine. In 1883 the Zerubavel society was founded in Odessa. It was named for the man who had led the Jews back to Eretz Yisrael from exile in Babylon in 536 B.C.E. This was the beginning of organized Zionism.

Surprisingly, in the same countries that had once given Jews equal rights—France, Germany, and Austria—people now began to speak and act against the Jews at this time. For example, in 1894 Alfred Dreyfus, an assimilated Jew and an officer in the French army, was falsely accused of betraying his country. He was found guilty and sentenced to life imprisonment. During his trial there were many expressions of anti-Semitism. Some people even wanted to take away the civil rights of the French Jews.

Theodor Herzl, a Viennese Jewish journalist at the trial, was amazed by how strong this anti-Semitism was. In his diary he wrote: "I have the solution to the Jewish problem. Not *a* solution, but *the* solution."

HERZL'S JEWISH STATE

Herzl said that even after the Jews of Western Europe were given equal rights, they were not allowed to become part of the society. In his book *The Jewish State* he said that the only solution was a Jewish state. He argued that anti-Semitism would hurt the European countries as well as the Jews, so these countries should help in establishing this Jewish state. Herzl held negotiations with Kaiser Wilhelm of Germany and the Turkish Sultan (then the ruler of Eretz Yisrael) in order to gain political benefits for the Jews. The Kaiser visited Eretz Yisrael in 1898, and in the same year Herzl went to Turkey to convince the Turkish ruler—the Sultan—to allow thousands of Jews to immigrate to Eretz Yisrael, but the Sultan would not agree.

Not all Jews agreed with Herzl. The wealthy ones whose help he needed thought he was crazy. Others were afraid that his ideas would encourage more anti-Semitism. But the members of Hovevei Zion were very enthusiastic. They promised to

Date	Locale and President	Important Resolutions and Events.
Aug. 29-31, 1897	Basle; Herzl	Founding of WZO and articulation of Basle Program.
Aug. 28-31, 1898	Basle; Herzl	Founding of Jewish Colonial Trust.
Aug. 15-18, 1899	Basle; Herzl	Ban on use of Zionist funds for activities outside Syria and Eretz Yisrael.
Aug. 13-16, 1900	London; Herzl	Agreement to work for improvement of Jewish life in Diaspora.
Aug. 26-30, 1901	Basle; Herzl	Founding of Jewish National Fund.
Aug. 23-28, 1903	Basle; Herzl	"Uganda Scheme."
July 27-Aug. 2, 1905	Basle; Wolffsohn	Rejection of "Uganda Scheme" and secession of Territorialists.
Aug. 14-21, 1907	The Hague; Wolffsohn	Presentation of "synthetic" Zionism which stressed Eretz Yisrael as only place where Zionism could be realized.
Aug. 26-30, 1909	Hamburg; Wolffsohn	Beginning of cooperative settlement in Eretz Yisrael as proposed by Oppenheimer.
Aug. 9-15, 1911	Basle; Warburg	Victory for "synthetic" Zionism; expansion of practical work in Eretz Yisrael.
Sept. 2-9, 1913	Vienna; Warburg	Decision to establish Hebrew University of Jerusalem and make immigration obligatory.
Sept. 1-14, 1921	Karlsbad; Weizmann	Belfour Declaration and British Mandate accepted; appeal for agreement with Arabs.

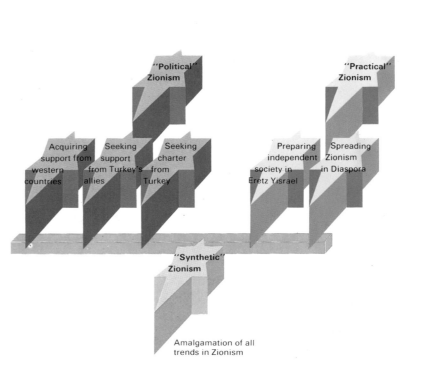

help him and wanted Herzl to become their leader.

In the summer of 1897, the First Zionist Congress took place in Basle, Switzerland. There were delegates from all over the world. They discussed the Jewish problem and stated their solution to it in the Basle program: "Zionism seeks to establish a home for the Jewish people in Eretz Yisrael under public law." They decided to send farmers and skilled workers to Eretz Yisrael, to strengthen Jewish national identity, and to start to get the international agreement to establish a Jewish state. They founded the World Zionist Organization and elected Herzl president. He remained the president until his death in 1904.

In 1903 the British suggested that the Jews settle in Uganda in East Africa. There were bitter arguments about this plan. Some people said that you could not have Zionism without Zion, and others saw Uganda as a place where the Jews would be safe until they had their own country. One of the notable opponents to the Uganda scheme was the Zionist leader Menachem Ussishkin. He believed that Zionists *must* live in Zion. In 1907, the Congress decided against Uganda. All their efforts were directed toward settling Jews in Eretz Yisrael.

The Zionist Congress was then like a Jewish parliament. It began to organize the institutions that the future Jewish state would need, and tried to convince the countries of the world to help the Jews establish their own state.

Left: A summary of the Zionist Congresses from 1897 to 1921.

Right: Stages in the fulfillment of the Basle Program up to 1914.

Menahem Ussishkin, a Zionist leader.

15

THE BEGINNING OF ZIONIST SETTLEMENT

Jerusalem is shown below in this copper engraving from 1657. The Temple mount is in the center.

The holy sites around Safed are shown in the guidebook below right. Mentioned in the book are places where, according to tradition, the sages were buried more than a thousand years earlier.

Below: A medallion from the 18th century showing Doña Gracia Nasi-Mendes. She supported the Jewish community in Tiberias.

For four hundred years Eretz Yisrael was part of the Ottoman Empire. It began in 1516, when the area was conquered by the Muslim Mamelukes, and ended in 1918—when the Empire collapsed in World War I, and the British conquered the country. Jewish settlement in Eretz Yisrael flourished only at the beginning of this period—mainly in the town of Safed in the Galilee, and toward the end—when Zionist settlement started.

In the 16th century, many Jews who had been expelled from Spain came to Eretz Yisrael. They settled in the old cities of Jerusalem, Gaza, Hebron, Tiberias, and especially in Safed.

The Jewish community in Safed at that time numbered about fifteen thousand. In this town the great *Halakhists* (sages who explained the Talmudic Laws), poets, and Kabbalists (sages who were engaged in Jewish mysticism) gathered. It was there that Joseph Caro wrote his book the *Shulhan Arukh* ("Prepared Table" in Hebrew), which was accepted as a law-book in Jewish communities of the Islamic countries. Jews who did not devote themselves to study worked in trade, weaving and dyeing. Silk and wool fabrics, which Safed exported from the port of Acre, were renowned throughout Europe.

Another Galilean town which enjoyed a short period of Jewish settlement was Tiberias. Well-known persons who helped this community included Doña Gracia Nasi-Mendes and her nephew Don Joseph Nasi. Doña Gracia was the daughter of a wealthy family from Portugal, who lived in the Netherlands. She was engaged in commerce and in smuggling of *anusim* (Jews who were forced to convert to Christianity) out of Spain and Portugal. She was also known for her generosity and for the charitable projects she established. In 1558 she and Don Joseph Nasi received the Ottoman Sultan's permission to lease Tiberias. They wanted to restore the city and turn it into a haven for exiles from Spain.

Toward the end of the 16th century many Jews left the Galilee because life there became very difficult; as under the rule of the Ottoman Empire, people had to pay huge taxes. Many villagers who were not able to pay the taxes were forced to abandon the land, which was then taken over by nomads and robbers. In the Galilean cities, trade declined and many people left. An earthquake in 1837 put an end to the remaining Jewish settlement in the Galilee.

In the 17th century, Jerusalem replaced Safed as the leading Jewish settlement, but for a short time only. Here, too, the residents suffered from heavy taxes and persecution. Life became almost unbearable for the Jews, and many left Eretz Yisrael. By the end of the century, only about 1,200 Jews were left in the city. But even in these hard times, Jews who believed in redemption still came to the Land of Israel, and many settled in Jerusalem. They lived on donations given by Jewish communities in the Diaspora. Thus, in the first half of the 19th century, fewer than 9,000 Jews lived in Eretz Yisrael, most of them in Jerusalem.

AT THE TURN OF THE CENTURY

At the end of the 18th century, the major European powers—Britain, France, Germany, and Russia— became interested in the Middle East, and especially in Eretz Yisrael. Napoleon tried to capture it from the Turks in 1799, but did not succeed. About 60 years later, the Suez Canal opened for shipping. It shortened the way from Europe to the Far East. This put Eretz Yisrael at the gateway of the trade routes to the Far East, and its importance grew. The European powers were waiting for the Ottoman Empire to collapse, so they could divide its territories among themselves. In the meantime, they encouraged charitable and religious good works in Eretz Yisrael, and in this way they gained some power in the region. Many churches, schools, and hospitals were built in the country, most of them in Jerusalem.

Jerusalem had now become the largest Jewish center in Eretz Yisrael. By the end of the 19th century, its Jewish population numbered 35,000—more than half of the city's total population. Jewish life in Jerusalem revolved around the synagogues and the Jewish religious Academies (the *yeshivot*). Secular schools for both boys and girls were also opened, all of which taught trades and general studies. Also during this time, the first Jewish neighborhood outside the walls of the Old City of Jerusalem was built. It was made up of long rows of buildings with iron gates for protection. It was considered dangerous to live there, and in order

A Turkish document from 1791, above, which deals with the taxes imposed on the residents of Jerusalem.

Jerusalem and its Holy Places, below far left. An illustration from the 19th century.

Below left is a painted-glass picture of Turkish soldiers, which decorated the Scroll of the Book of Esther. Probably the work of Joseph Geiger of Safed, 1893.

The Italian Hospital and Church, bottom far left, were built in Jerusalem in the early 20th century.

Below: The first Jewish neighborhood outside the walls of the Old City of Jerusalem.

The philanthropist Sir Moses Montefiore (1784–1885) above.

Center: Baron Rothschild, on the right, with clerks.

The settlement Mazkeret ("in memory of") Batyah, above right, was founded in 1885 and is named after the mother of Baron Rothschild.

Right: Early days at Deganya, the first agricultural communal settlement.

to encourage settlement, rent-free houses were offered. The new quarter outside the walls was built with the help of Sir Moses Montefiore, a Jewish philanthropist and humanitarian from England. Montefiore met with the Turkish Sultan on behalf of the Jews and worked to establish other Jewish settlements in Eretz Yisrael.

THE BEGINNING OF ZIONISM IN ERETZ YISRAEL

The year 1881 was a turning point in Jewish immigration to Eretz Yisrael. Most of the immigrants who arrived after that time believed that a national homeland for the Jews would put an end to their suffering. These immigrants are called *olim,* and an act of immigration is called *Aliyah,* from the Hebrew word *la-alot* which means to ascend, or to go up.

Immigrants arrived in Eretz Yisrael in waves, and each group had its own special character.

During the First Aliyah, a wave of immigration which lasted from 1881 to 1903, 70,000 Jewish immigrants (olim) came to Eretz Yisrael. Most of them were members of the *Hovevei Zion* ("Lovers of Zion") movement in eastern Europe, who had fled from the riots there. A few came from central Europe and from Islamic countries. Conditions were hard and only about half of these olim decided to stay. Of these, a few believed that the return to Zion should mean a

return to the land, and they set up farming settlements. However, they met with many difficulties. The Ottoman government, afraid of too many people coming to Eretz Yisrael from enemy countries, made buying land and settling difficult. Also, the settlers were not familiar with the climate, the country, and its farming methods. They bought lands which were not suitable for either farming or settling, and so they suffered from starvation, poverty, and malaria.

Help came to the pioneers from the French Jewish Baron Edmond de Rothschild, nicknamed "The Well-Known Benefactor." He sent agricultural experts who brought in dozens of new crops such as tea, cotton, and tobacco. He based much of the farming on citrus groves, and he improved work methods. The Baron's support saved the Zionist settlement project in Eretz Yisrael, and laid the groundwork for additional settlements.

Most of the olim settled in the city of Jaffa, which was the center of Jewish life in those days. The

Hebrew language, which was the only language common to them all, could now be heard in the street, at home, and in school.

The Second Aliyah (1904–1914) was made up mainly of immigrants who had left Russia after the pogroms of 1903 and 1905 and the unsuccessful Socialist Revolution of 1905. As in the First Aliyah, most of this group turned to the cities, and in 1909 the first all-Jewish city was founded—Tel Aviv. Its name was derived from the Hebrew words for the title of Theodor Herzl's book *Altneuland.*

At first, it was intended as a pretty Jewish suburb with gardens near Jaffa. Loans were provided to the residents by the Jewish National Fund on the condition that all construction and development be done by Jewish laborers. The area developed quickly, and in 1914 it boasted 1000 inhabitants. Within two decades Tel Aviv became the largest city in Eretz Yisrael.

Some of the olim dreamed of creating an ideal society, one which would be a mixture of national rebirth and social revolution. One group of these pioneers set up Deganya, the first agricultural commune. Its members lived lives of sharing and equality and did all the work themselves. Another group founded the *Ha-Shomer* ("The Guard") organization. These were men and women who believed in guarding the new Jewish settlements themselves. Members of Ha-Shomer were given orders to either go out to work or to perform guard duty, because labor and guard duty were intertwined. They operated as "conquest units" whose task was to prevent lands purchased by Jewish money from being tilled by Arabs (thus establishing ownership rights). Hence it was they who established the borders of Jewish settlement. They realized their dream of combining labor, defense, and

Left: Jewish workers in vineyards, 1910.

Below: Members of Ha-Shomer (The Guard) in Arab dress, with modern weapons.

settlement, by establishing Ha-Shomer settlements—Moshav Tel Adashim and Kibbutz Kefar Giladi.

In order to be accepted as a member of Ha-Shomer, applicants had to pass stringent tests, in which they had to prove their courage, resourcefulness, and levelheadedness. Helping a friend in trouble—even if it involved risking one's own life—was an imperative, and use of weapons was permitted only as a last resort.

Other immigrants organized themselves into work-groups; they

"Tel Aviv, Small White Houses amidst the Sand Dunes"—*a painting from 1923 by Reuven Rubin (1898–1980).*

tried to prove to the Jewish farmers who owned orange groves and vineyards that they were just as good as the Arab workers, and that the farmers should employ them instead.

The number of Jews living in Eretz Yisrael had grown from 24,000, at the beginning of Zionist activity, to 85,000. The land for settlement was bought mainly by the Jewish National Fund, which was established in 1901 to make the lands of Eretz Yisrael the property of the Jewish people and to develop them for forests and settlements.

Britain Gains Control

World War I broke out in June 1914. The Allied countries of Britain, France, and Russia fought against the Axis powers of Germany and Austro-Hungary, which were later joined by Turkey. Each of the countries involved desired to

conquer other areas and to firmly secure its power.

The Jews of Eretz Yisrael suffered under the harsh and corrupt Turkish rule, and many longed for the fall of the Ottoman Empire. Some of those who actively worked to this end belonged to a spy ring, called Nili (Hebrew initials for "the Eternal One of Israel will not lie"). Led by brother and sister Aaron and Sarah Aaronsohn, they gained the support of the British. There were many Jewish settlers, however, who felt that Nili's activities endangered the new settlements.

The British had been waiting for years for the Ottoman Empire to collapse. They wanted to secure their own rule over the area, and they signed a number of agreements hoping to achieve this. One, the secret Sykes-Picot Agreement of 1916, planned to divide the Middle East between Britain and France if and when the Turks were defeated, placing the central part of Eretz Yisrael, from the Lower Galilee to Beersheba, under international control. At the same time, Britain's high commissioner in Egypt, Sir Henry McMahon, promised Sherif Hussein of Mecca, of the Hashemite dynasty, that Britain would recognize an Arab kingdom under his rule. In return, Britain asked the Arabs to revolt against Turkey, and then recognize British rule over certain parts of the Middle East. This, and other similar promises Britain made to the Arabs, would frequently clash with Zionist interests in the future.

The Zionist leaders in England during World War I were headed by Nahum Sokolow and Chaim Weizmann. They pinned their hopes on a British victory and felt that the war gave Zionism a unique opportunity. They tried to persuade the British leaders that they would gain politically by supporting the Zionist cause. Chaim Weizmann

(1874–1952), who was later appointed the first president of the State of Israel, lectured in chemistry at the University of Manchester. Thanks to his scientific work, which helped the British war effort, he was appointed to a senior position in the Admiralty laboratories. Thus he was able to influence the British leaders.

Weizmann proposed to the British government that it officially declare its support of the Zionist Movement,

Zionists had been hoping for—recognition of Eretz Yisrael as the national home of the Jewish people. Nevertheless, it meant international recognition—which the Zionist Federation had been working for ever since the First Zionist Congress in 1897. Despite its conservative wording, the Balfour Declaration inspired new hope in the Jewish people and was received with joy in Eretz Yisrael.

which it did in 1917. The British Declaration was written as a personal letter from Lord Arthur James Balfour to Lionel Walter Rothschild, who played an important role in the discussions.

The Balfour Declaration recognized the right of the Jewish people to build their national home in Palestine, and supported the rights of the non-Jewish residents as well as the rights of Jews in other countries. It was not what the

The British army, led by General Edmund Allenby, arrived at the gates of Jerusalem in December 1917. The British conquest of Eretz Yisrael was completed in September 1918, and a British military government was established. In July 1920, the new League of Nations gave Britain control over Palestine, on the condition that it help to establish the Jewish National Home and carry out the Balfour Declaration.

Top: Chaim Weizmann, who was the president of the World Zionist Organization. In 1948 he was chosen the first president of Israel.

Above: The Golden Book *of the Jewish National Fund, made by Meir Gur-Aryeh in 1913. Generous donors were inscribed in this book.*

71

16

TOWARD THE NEW WORLD

The statue shown below far right was erected in Chicago to honor Robert Morris (left) and Haym Salomon (right), whose financial support to the Revolutionary Army was crucial to the winning of American independence. George Washington is in the center.

The first synagogue in America was built in New York in 1730 on Old Mill Street (today South William Street), which then became known as "Jews' Alley."

Abigail-Bilha, right, was the wife of Jacob Franks, head of the influential family who came from England in 1708–1709. David Salisbury Franks (in the picture above) became a colonel in the Revolutionary Army.

Over five and a half million Jews live in the United States today, more than in any other country in the world. How did the first Jews reach America? How did their number grow into the millions in just 300 years?

ORIGINS

The first Jews to arrive in America were forced converts (*anusim*) of Spanish and Portuguese origin who had gone to live in Brazil, and from there moved to the Dutch colony of New Amsterdam in 1654. About ten years later, the English took control of America's eastern seaboard, and New Amsterdam became New York. Jewish families now arrived from England along with the British army, and from central and eastern Europe. Six communities were established in the Colonies: in Newport, R.I.; New York; Philadelphia; Charleston, S.C.; Savannah, Georgia; and Richmond, Virginia.

During the American Revolution, a large majority of Jews in the Colonies supported the rebellion

against the British. Some fought in the war, and even rose to high rank in the military. Others provided financial support to the Revolutionary Army. Haym Salomon of Philadelphia, for example, had come from Poland only four years before the Revolution. Because of his selfless aid to the American cause, he died bankrupt, but greatly admired for his devotion to freedom.

When the Colonies became independent in 1776, there were about 2,000 Jews living there. The Bill of Rights, added to the Constitution in 1791, promised freedom of religion for all, which, of course, meant equal rights for the Jews too.

During the 19th century, many Jews came to the United States from central and western Europe. The number of Jews in America grew from 5,000 in 1826 to 280,000 in 1880.

The immigrants started out as

peddlers or small-businessmen. As trade and travel moved westward, large Jewish communities started in

Cleveland, Chicago, Detroit, Milwaukee, and Cincinnati. The Jews' economic situation slowly improved. A typical example might be that of the peddler, who bought a wagon, and then a shop, and over the years the shop became a chain of stores. By the time of the Civil War—in which about 10,000 Jews fought (7,000 with the North)— some of the famous bankers and industrialists in America were Jews, most of them originally from Germany. The Seligman banking house strongly supported the North in the war. Afterwards, their bank continued to act as the official monetary agent for the U.S. government and Department of the Navy. In 1869, President Grant even offered one of the brothers, Joseph Seligman, the post of secretary of the treasury, but Seligman declined.

Most of the wealthy Jews in the late 19th and early 20th century are

joined the Reform movement. Reform Judaism was brought to the United States in the mid-19th century by Jews from central Europe. The first Reform congregation in America was established by Rabbi Isaac Mayer Wise in Cincinnati in 1854.

Reform Jews believe that Judaism means *only* belief in God and in the Jewish moral principles. They do not accept the traditional behavior that is dictated by the Halakhah—the religious laws—and they say most of the prayers in English instead of Hebrew. Reform Judaism also encourages integration into the local society. And most of the Jewish immigrants wanted very much to become a part of American life.

SHAPING THE JEWISH COMMUNITY

By the late 1920s, there were already more Jews in America than

Below far left: The Reform Movement's Hebrew Union College was founded in Cincinnati, Ohio, in 1873.

Below center: Jewish immigrants from Russia, in a painting by Ben Shahn dated 1941. It is based on a photograph taken in 1906, the high point of Jewish immigration.

remembered more for their charitable activities than for their business successes. Julius Rosenwald, for example, started as an apprentice in his uncle's clothing store, and within nine years owned one quarter of Sears, Roebuck and Co. He devoted a large portion of his fortune to providing agricultural and educational aid to the blacks of America. Jacob H. Schiff, Otto Kahn, Solomon Guggenheim, and Felix M. Warburg were famous patrons of the arts, and helped establish and maintain museums, orchestras, and opera houses.

During this period, many Jews

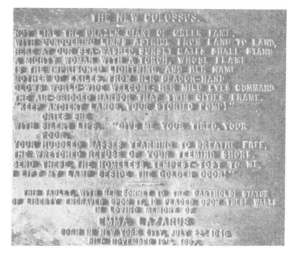

in any other country in the world. From 1880 to 1929, their number grew to about four and a half million. Most of them came from

Many Jewish immigrants earned their living by peddling and selling. This sketch above comes from a matchbox dating from the end of the 19th century.

Emma Lazarus, whose moving poem, left, is inscribed on a tablet in the entrance to the Statue of Liberty, worked tirelessly to help the poor and homeless immigrants. Her own family had come to the United States in Colonial times.

Russia because it was so difficult for them to earn a living there, and because of the anti-Semitism.

The majority of these immigrants lived in the industrial cities of the east and midwest, especially in New York City. At first they joined relatives or former neighbors, so they stayed close together in cheap, crowded neighborhoods. On New York's Lower East Side, for example, about 350,000 Jews lived in an area of only 6 square kilometers (2.5 square miles). They spoke Yiddish and most of them lived some form of traditional Jewish life. Cultural activities were very important. There were daily, weekly, and monthly Yiddish newspapers, as well as literature, theater, classes, radio programs, and films.

The more established settlers were employed in commerce, finance, and the academic professions; but most of the newcomers in New York worked in the garment industry which was owned mainly by Jewish businessmen. They worked 70 hours a week in dark, crowded rooms (known as "sweatshops" because of the terrible heat and hard work). Some Jewish leaders organized the workers to fight for better conditions. They founded the Jewish labor unions. This was actually the beginning of the labor movement in America.

Eventually, many of the second and third generation of immigrants changed their occupations. They moved to different cities and states, and soon became part of American society. As they did so, many of them went less often to the synagogue, and sent their children to public schools. Some of the children went to Hebrew classes for a few hours a week, but many had no regular Jewish education. In response to this, the Conservative movement was established by people who wanted to preserve their Jewish traditions. Laypeople, such as Schiff and Warburg, supported Solomon Schechter in his efforts to integrate the Eastern European Jewish masses into the American way of Life.

Conservative Judaism, with its innovations (such as sermons in English instead of Yiddish), seemed less foreign to the American spirit than Orthodox Judaism, but more traditional than Reform. It tries to adapt the religious laws to the needs of modern society. And, although many Jews no longer lived traditionally Jewish lives, they still felt close to Eretz Yisrael; so the Zionist movement, too, found its place in America.

During World War I, there were

about a quarter of a million Jews in the American army, and more than 3,000 died in battle. After the war, there was a spirit of isolationism and nationalism in America. From 1921 to 1924, laws were passed that limited immigration into the United States from all countries except North European ones. This also meant there were fewer Jewish immigrants from central and eastern Europe. At this time, some unwritten quotas were imposed by many social clubs and universities for Jews and other minorities. The American political leaders and intellectuals opposed this anti-Semitism, although it was never on the scale of the ingrained anti-

America and abroad, and to help the refugees who left Europe when anti-Semitism there grew stronger, especially in Nazi Germany.

In 1939, before World War II began, almost five million Jews lived in the United States, about one third of all the Jewish people in the world. By now, they were well-established and many had made names for themselves in practically every field, in business, scholarship, medicine, the arts, and entertainment. There were Jewish musicians, like Irving Berlin and Benny Goodman; Hollywood producers, like Louis B. Mayer and the four Warner brothers; poets, like Emma Lazarus, whose poem,

The Isaac Mayer Wise Reform Synagogue in Cincinnati, Ohio, shown below center.

Temple Emanuel, shown below, a Reform temple in New York which was built in 1868.

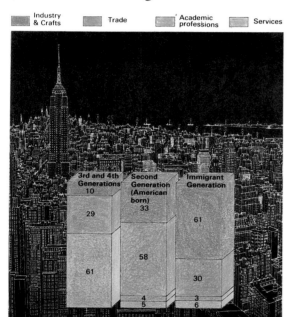

| Industry & Crafts | Trade | Academic professions | Services |

Year	New England	Central Atlantic Coast	Southern Atlantic Coast	North Central East	North Central West	South Central East	South Central West	Mountain Region	Pacific Coast (incl. Hawaii and Alaska)	Total
1878	11.8	104.3	21.9	36.4	10.1	11.7	12.3	2.0	19.7	230.2
1907	131.0	1,125.0	75.5	238.0	80.0	30.3	32.1	11.2	53.6	1,776.7
1927	355.4	2,534.2	177.2	672.6	166.6	61.3	79.7	30.1	151.1	4,228.2
1955	334.3	3,035.5	291.0	576.8	138.2	37.7	74.6	36.8	449.3	4,974.2
1980	372.1	2,886.1	779.4	532.9	130.0	38.8	94.5	97.2	759.0	5,690.0

Semitism of Europe.

The economic crisis of 1929 hit the American Jewish community as hard as everyone else in the country. But some people still blamed the Jews. In response, the American Jewish community drew closer together. The Jews united during the 1930s to fight anti-Semitism both in

"The New Colossus," is inscribed on a tablet on the Statue of Liberty; and athletes, like the baseball player Hank Greenberg and the boxer Max Baer who held the heavyweight title in 1934. Like other immigrant groups before and after them, the Jews had fully integrated into American life.

Over the years, many Jews moved out of the cities, primarily to the south, the west, and the southwest. The table shows the Jewish population in various areas of the U.S.A. (in thousands). The colors in the table correspond to the colors in the map.

17
BUILDING IN ERETZ YISRAEL

Below: Yehoshua Hankin (1864–1945), called the "Redeemer of the Land," with his wife Olga. Under his initiative a total of about 150,000 acres of land in Eretz Yisrael was purchased for Jewish settlements.

A cooperative labor battalion paving roads in 1925.

The years between World War I and World War II (1919–1939) were also the years of British rule in Eretz Yisrael, then called Palestine. The Mandate, confirmed by the League of Nations on July 24, 1922, provided that the British would facilitate the establishment of institutions of self-government by the Jewish population in Eretz Yisrael. During that time the population of the Jews tripled, and more than 60 new settlements were founded.

IMMIGRATION AND SETTLEMENT

The people who came between 1919 and 1923 are known as the Third Aliyah. Most of them came from Russia and were members of the *He-Halutz* ("Pioneer") movement. The movement was founded between 1915 and 1917 by Joseph Trumpeldor in Russia and by David Ben-Gurion (later the first prime minister of Israel) and Itzhak Ben-Zvi (Israel's second president) in the United States. They wanted to establish a Zionist-Socialist center in Eretz Yisrael. Before immigrating to Eretz Yisrael, they learned farming methods and Hebrew, and when they reached Palestine, they established new farming settlements.

Some of these immigrants settled in the rapidly growing cities. Many of them established cooperatives and took jobs paving roads, in construction, and in manufacturing.

There were 93,000 Jews in Eretz Yisrael in 1923. During the next 18 months, 48,000 more arrived. The majority of them came from Eastern Europe, and 12 percent came from Yemen and Iraq. Most of these

immigrants of the Fourth Aliyah (1924–1931) settled in the cities. Tel Aviv grew very rapidly at this time.

The citrus industry was now developed, and became one of the major branches of the country's economy.

The next decade, 1929–1939, held years of strong growth. The Jewish population in Eretz Yisrael grew

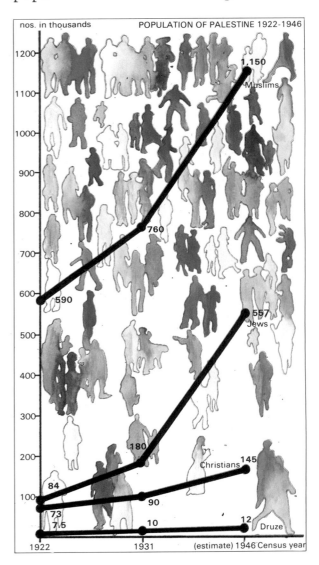

from 175,000 in 1931 to 475,000 in 1939. About 230,000 immigrants—the Fifth Aliyah—arrived mostly from Germany. It was the Nazi rise to power in Germany in 1933 that convinced them to leave. Most of

the countries in the western world locked their gates to the Jews, so Palestine was almost the only place they could go. In order to rescue these people, Chaim Weizmann, then the president of the World Zionist Federation, and Arthur Ruppin together founded the Central Office for Settling the Jews of Germany. Another organization, Youth Aliyah, brought thousands of children to Palestine during this period.

VIOLENCE IN PALESTINE

From the very first, the Arabs opposed Zionist settlement in Palestine. They felt the Jews were encroaching on their land, where they had lived for generations. In 1891, 100 Arab notables from Jerusalem demanded that the Ottoman government forbid Jews to immigrate to Eretz Yisrael or purchase land in the country. After the Balfour Declaration, when the British recognized the right of the Jews to a home in Eretz Yisrael, Zionism was felt to be a real threat by the Arabs, and their opposition grew stronger. In February 1919, the Arab states sent representatives to a congress in Syria. They demanded that the Zionist claims be rejected. Zionist claims be rejected.

A year later Arab forces attacked Jewish settlements in the Galilee.

The settlements were evacuated and many brave people, including Joseph Trumpeldor, were killed trying to defend them. Another Arab mob attacked the Jewish quarter in Jerusalem. The British appointed Sir Herbert Samuel, a Zionist Jew, as high commissioner for Palestine, and this angered the Arabs even more.

The local Arabs now began to call themselves "Palestinians." They tried to convince the British not to allow the Jews to establish a national home in Eretz Yisrael. They wanted a Palestinian Arab government instead. When the British rejected their demands, the 1921 May Day parade in Jaffa turned into a riot.

Because of this violence, the British limited the number of Jews who could immigrate to Palestine, but they did not give the Arabs what they really wanted—an end to the Jewish national home.

The religious and political leader of the Arabs in Palestine was the Mufti Haj Amin al-Husseini. He wanted an all-out attack on the Jews and the British, so he told the Arabs that the Jews were a danger to the Muslim holy places on the Temple Mount. In August 1929, there were bloody Arab riots in Jerusalem that soon spread to the rest of the country. These riots were larger and more violent than ever before. At Hebron and Safed, Jews were

Below: The Roaring Lion *memorial to Trumpeldor and his comrades, who were killed in 1920 defending Tel-Hai from Arab attack.*

In the massacre in Hebron in August 1929, Arabs brutally murdered helpless Jews. Above: a ransacked home.

The map at right shows the purchase of land in Palestine by Jews.

Far right: Maps of the plan to divide Palestine between the Arabs and the Jews. Note how much smaller the Jewish area (brown) is in the plan from 1938 than in the plan from 1937.

brutally murdered, and several small, isolated Jewish settlements had to be abandoned.

Nevertheless, the Jewish settlement in Palestine grew rapidly during the 1930s. The Arabs wanted more than ever to put an end to Zionist hopes. In 1936, they started a campaign of violence and terror against the Jews and the British in Palestine known as the Riots of 1936–1939. They began in Jaffa in April 1936 and spread throughout the country. Hundreds of people were killed or wounded, and

Nahariya

Haifa

Nazareth

Mediterranean Sea

Netanyah

Tel Aviv

Jerusalem

• Gaza

Dead Sea

Beersheba

0 10 20
└──┴──┴──┘ km

· Lands owned by Jews in 1929
Lands purchased by Jews in 1929–1936

thousands of acres of fields and orchards were destroyed. In order to paralyze the economic life of the country, the Arab High Committee declared a general strike. For 175 days, no Arab reported for work and all Arab-owned companies remained closed. The Arabs compelled the Jews to speed up production. Within

a short time, Ben-Gurion could declare: "The Arab strike does not threaten our economic survival. On the contrary, our economic independence has grown."

In August 1937, a commission was appointed in London to investigate the causes of the riots and to suggest some solutions. The commission recommended that the country be divided between the Arabs and the Jews. The Arabs rejected this, and more violence erupted. The main targets were now British soldiers and army camps. The British

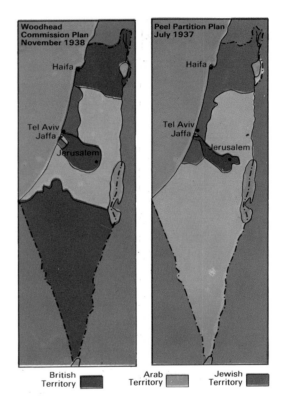

Woodhead Commission Plan November 1938

Haifa

Tel Aviv
Jaffa

Jerusalem

Peel Partition Plan July 1937

Haifa

Tel Aviv
Jaffa

Jerusalem

British Territory   Arab Territory   Jewish Territory

responded by declaring the Arab High Committee illegal and arrested many of its members.

England, however, wanted a peaceful compromise in Palestine. In 1939, just before World War II, the British government invited representatives of the Jewish Agency and the Arab states to a round table conference in London. They had to meet with each side separately, because the Arabs refused to sit together with the Jews and were not willing to compromise at all. The British gave in to the Arabs and issued new regulations that greatly limited Jewish immigration and

Far left: The Jewish constables in the British police force helped put down the riots and defend the settlements. Officially they were British policemen, but secretly they were all members of the Haganah Jewish defense force.

Stockade and Tower Settlement, left, was painted by Zionah Tadjar. The tower was raised and a wooden fence built. The settlers lived in tents and huts.

Above top photo: Women were full partners in labor and defense from the earliest days of Zionist settlement. Here they help build the tower and stockade settlement of Hanita in 1938.

The Aviron ("airplane") Company was founded in 1936. It was the "air force" of the Haganah. Shown above are members of the first flight course in 1937.

settlement and made it very difficult for the Jews to defend themselves; so the Jews decided to fight the British, both with weapons and by gaining international political support.

THE JEWISH RESPONSE

The *Haganah* ("Defense" in Hebrew) organization was established in 1920 as a response to the Arab attacks on Jewish citizens. It was to be the army of the Jewish community.

During the riots of 1929, the Jews realized that the British would not protect them. When the British also began to limit Jewish immigration to Palestine and to forbid Jews to purchase land in the country, many more people realized the importance of an independent Jewish defense force. By 1937, about 25,000 men and women were members of the Haganah.

When the Arabs began to attack the British in 1936, the British decided to accept help from the Jews. They expanded the Jewish police force, and a British officer, Charles Orde Wingate, started to train special Jewish brigades to fight the Arab terrorists. Wingate was called "The Friend" because of his strong support for Zionism—and

this was the reason his superiors in the British army transferred him from Palestine.

The purpose of the Arab riots of 1936–1939 was to destroy Jewish settlements in Palestine. But the opposite happened. Despite the British limitations on immigration, 86,000 new immigrants reached Eretz Yisrael at this time. Most of them had to come illegally.

New settlements were now set up in places that were chosen very carefully. They were established where they could prevent Arab attacks, enable the Jews to defend themselves, and ensure that important areas would be in the Jewish state if the British decided to divide the country between the Arabs and the Jews. During this time, about 50 new settlements were established literally overnight. They were called "stockade and tower" settlements, because these were the two structures that were built during the night—a fence for protection and a watchtower. This period of growth and new settlement ended in 1939, when the British issued new regulations against immigration. World War II began that same year.

18
UNDER THE TERROR OF THE SWASTIKA

By the middle of the 19th century, people in Europe had begun to have certain ideas about different races and nationalities. Anthropology, the science which studies the development of the human race, divided people into races according to physical characteristics such as skin color and body measurements. In 1853 the French writer Gubino published a book in which he argued that the different human races were not equal. He divided people into three races: white, yellow, and black, and claimed that the white was superior. He also said that among the white races, the Aryans (those from northern Europe) were the best.

Scholars, too, claimed that there was a connection between a man's race and his characteristics and abilities. Biologists declared that

nature had evolved over hundreds of thousands of years from a primitive and lowly state to more developed forms. This idea was formulated by the Englishman Charles Darwin, who wrote the book *Origin of Species* in 1859. His Theory of Evolution introduced to the world such ideas as "natural selection," "survival of the fittest," and "war of survival"—which really means the victory of the "strong," the "superior," and the "successful," and the destruction of all the others. Hatred of the Jews soon became based on this new branch of "science."

RACIAL ANTI-SEMITISM
Modern "racial" anti-Semites did not see the Jews so much as a religious, social, or economic problem, but as opponents in a contest between

"The Wandering Jew," *at right, an illustration by Doré (1852). The idea of the wandering Jew came from the Christian legend of a Jew who humiliated Jesus on his way to the crucifixion and was therefore doomed to eternal wandering.*

Far right: "Come, children, have some candy, but in return you must come with me"—a cartoon of the anti-Semitic view of the Jew who entices small children.

races—a struggle for survival. They considered the Jewish people an inferior race, and they feared Jews who had converted even more than

Jews who had kept their religion. In time, racial anti-Semitism led to a feeling that Jews should be removed from humanity. The Jew was described by anti-Semits as a member of a separate "anti-race," actually related to a microbe ("Bacillus Judaicus").

Anti-Semitism spread fast in Europe in the second half of the 19th century. It became a part of the culture—in music, theater, literature, painting, sculpture, language, and even popular games. There were many reasons for this. One reason was that the industrial revolution caused many people to feel unsure of themselves in their own societies. The working class suffered from poverty and unemployment, which made them open to ideas that promised to deliver them from their suffering. The Jews were convenient scapegoats.

Another reason was the increasing participation of often uneducated masses in the political system. Unscrupulous politicians made unrealistic promises in order to get their votes. The way was prepared, therefore, for extreme ideas like anti-Semitism to catch on. The Jews hoped that anti-Semitism would eventually fade away, but it was soon obvious that a new and more violent anti-Semitism was developing. And this, in turn, led to the greatest disaster to befall the Jewish people in their entire history—the Nazi Holocaust.

Nazi Anti-Semitic Policy

The shock of defeat in World War I and the harsh terms imposed on Germany by the Treaty of Versailles prepared the way for the rise of the National Socialist German Workers' Party—the Nazi party.

The Treaty of Versailles was signed in the Palace of Versailles near Paris on the 28th of June, 1919, between the powers who won the war—America, France, and Britain—and the countries who lost —Japan and Italy. In addition to having its territories taken away, Germany was made to pay high war-reparations. The Kaiser and the generals, who led the country during the war, fled or were forced to resign. The new government had to accept the conditions of the Treaty of Versailles. Life for the German people became very hard: unemployment was high, and even those who did have work did not earn enough to live on. Other countries felt that in order to help Europe get back on its feet, they had better help Germany overcome its economic difficulties. And so, with the intervention of the United States, Germany's terms of payment were made easier. With the help of big loans, Germany began to rebuild itself.

But in 1929 the U.S.A. suffered an economic crisis. The crisis spread to Europe and Germany, in particular,

That the Jews were scheming to take over the world, portrayed below left, was one of the main arguments used in anti-Semitic propaganda (Vienna, 1912).

Below: In this 1920 election poster, the Jew is depicted as a deadly snake strangling the country. Sums of money are written on his body to symbolize Jewish capitalism, while beside him are the hammer and sickle, symbols of Jewish Bolshevism. The caption reads: "Save Austria!"

Above: In these two entries taken from a British dictionary of synonyms published as recently as 1957, the word "Jew" has meaning in two negative contexts: moneylending and greed.

Right: "Do not buy from Jews," a sign in Berlin.

Far right: A chart of the Nuremberg Laws, from 1935. They defined a Jew as a person who had at least three Jewish grandparents, or who had two Jewish grandparents and was married to a Jew. Later, a Jew was defined as any person with even one Jewish grandparent.

Die Nürnberger Gesetze

The photograph above shows Heinrich Himmler, center, and Reinhard Heydrich, chief of the Reich Security Main Office, on right.

suffered. Unemployment rose daily, the value of money dropped, and throughout Germany the distress increased. The government changed hands many times but could not pull the country out of the crisis. Within this maze of hardship, Hitler succeeded in captivating the masses. He promised the people a stable government, work, and security. He promised to return to them their German honor which they had lost in the war, namely to set up once again the great German realm (the German Reich). This meant taking control over the neighboring countries, and then over all of Europe.

Hitler was appointed prime minister (Chancellor) on June 30th, 1933, although his Nazi party did not have a majority in the German Parliament (the Reichstag). On the very next day, the brownshirts—the S.A. or "stormtroopers"—of the Nazi party, with the swastika as their symbol, ran amok in the streets, violently attacking, murdering, and plundering. Their victims, though mainly Jews, also included socialists, communists and democrats.

Four weeks later, the Reichstag building was burned down. This gave the Nazis an excuse for passing a law which took away from the Jews their freedom of speech and freedom to congregate. Elections

were held in an atmosphere of fear and terror. The Nazis won a majority. The swastika became the symbol of Germany, and the Nazi party was the only party allowed by law. Now the party could mobilize the S.S. unit and the Gestapo. The S.S. was a "defense unit" of the Nazi party. Those who were chosen to serve in it had to have Aryan features and show absolute loyalty to the party. At its head was Heinrich Himmler. The Gestapo was the "State Secret Police," which could deal with anyone opposing the rule in any way it saw fit. The Gestapo was above the law. Many people who were suspected of being enemies of the state were arrested, put in concentration camps, expelled, and murdered. A systematic persecution of Jews began. This was carried out in various ways. New laws were passed which gave the Jews an inferior status. The worst of these were the Nuremberg Laws, passed in September 1935, which made racism legal and stripped Jews of their German citizenship.

The Jews were also persecuted economically. They were dismissed from their jobs. Factory owners and merchants also suffered. Jewish businesses were taken away and placed in Aryan hands.

In addition to the laws and economic punishments, the Jews

were made to suffer psychologically as well. A campaign was launched which aimed at filling the entire German public with anti-Semitic feelings, and encouraged them to act out their anti-Semitic sentiments. This job was carried out by fanatic party men like Minister of Propaganda Josef Goebbels, and Julius Streicher, editor of the anti-Semitic paper *Der Stuermer.* In 1938 the anti-Jewish policy grew worse.

Left: The burned-out sanctuary of the Berlin synagogue after "Kristallnacht."

"He steals the soul, sucks the blood—beware of the Jews"—anti-Semitic Nazi propaganda on a street sign, below.

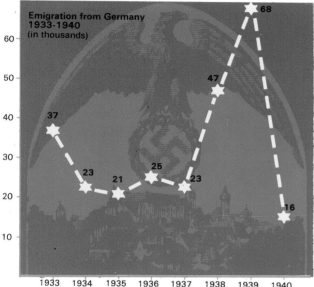

Chart far left: About half a million Jews were living in Germany in 1933. By 1939 about half had emigrated or had been expelled. From 1939 on, all Jews' passports were designed to make immigration more difficult.

Adolf Hitler at a Nazi party rally in 1936. The flags behind him bear the party's symbol—the swastika.

Germany annexed Austria (the "Anschluss") and much pressure was put on Jews to leave. In Vienna, Adolf Eichmann, head of the Jewish Section of the Gestapo, began to force Jews to emigrate. By the end of October, some 17,000 Polish Jews had been expelled from Germany.

Violence against the Jews reached a peak on "Kristallnacht" (November 9–10, 1938) or "Night of Broken Glass," so named because of the many windows smashed in synagogues and Jewish businesses. Hundreds were destroyed and set on fire, dozens of Jews were killed and thousands were arrested and imprisoned in camps. In January 1939, Hitler set up a special office in the Ministry of Interior called the "Reich Central Office for Jewish Emigration," which planned actions against the Jews. This marked the beginning of the phase which led to the "Final Solution" (to the so-called Jewish problem).

19
THE HOLOCAUST

The Magen David (Shield of David), or Jewish star, worn by a woman in Hungary.

Below right: Smuggling food into the ghetto became necessary to survive. Much of it was done by children.

The residents of an old-age home in Frankfurt, before being deported to Eastern Europe, shown bottom left.

The Warsaw ghetto children's chorus, bottom right.

The Nazi net began to tighten around the Jews. In September 1939, the German army invaded Poland in a lightning operation known as the "blitzkrieg." Millions of Jews now found themselves under Nazi rule. Emigration was no longer possible. Jews from the age of ten years and up had to wear a Jewish star (Magen David) pinned to their clothes. They were kept apart from their non-Jewish neighbors, and in eastern Europe they were removed from their towns and forced to live in special quarters in the big cities—the ghettos.

The ghettos were surrounded by well-guarded walls and fences. Only Jews who worked for Nazis were allowed out. Daily life in the various ghettos was extremely hard. The Jews suffered from hunger as the Germans allowed only a small amount of food to be brought into the ghetto. Food was smuggled in or bought on the black market and through bribery. The ghetto was dreadfully overcrowded. The Warsaw ghetto, for example, covered 2.4% of the area of the city, but held 30% of the city's population (450,000 people)! Several families had to live in a single apartment, and masses of people filled the streets. Despite many efforts to keep the ghetto clean and sanitary, disease and epidemics spread. Indeed, by the time all the Jews in the ghettos were transported to the death camps, hundreds of thousands had already died of hunger and disease.

Nonetheless, the Jewish people showed a strong will to live and great creative powers. Every ghetto organized schools and cultural and welfare activities. A children's choir, for example, was formed in the Warsaw ghetto. "Music in the ghetto? Songs in the cemetery? What sense was there in that?" Thus did I. Gurewitz, in his memoirs of the Vilna ghetto, describe the

debate over establishing an orchestra in the ghetto. And his answer was: "Together with the sounds of the orchestra, the hearts of the Jews were filled with an underlying sound which said: 'The Jewish people is alive!'"

The desire to keep alive their image as human beings, and as Jews in particular, was great. Here the synagogues played an important role, both as a place for spiritual uplift, and as a meeting place which gave a feeling of togetherness.

THE "FINAL SOLUTION"

In 1940 Germany also occupied Denmark, Norway, Belgium, and France. The Jews of these countries were now also sent east. The aim of the Germans in the beginning of Nazi rule was to "cleanse" Europe of Jews, but not necessarily to kill them. In 1941 the Nazis made the decision, while they were planning their war against "Bolshevist-Jewish" Russia, to actually murder all the Jews of Europe.

The Nazis used two main methods of killing Jews. The first was sending mobile death squads to kill victims not far from where they lived. These groups executed about 1.5 million Jews. The second method was to set up death camps to which victims would be brought from great distances. Such camps were built in eastern Poland and Russia—at Chelmno, Auschwitz-Birkenau, Treblinka, Sobibor, Belzec, and Majdanek. In these camps, special equipment for mass murder was set up: gas chambers disguised as showers, firing squads and burial pits, and crematoria for burning the corpses. About 4 million people were murdered in the camps. The Jews were usually rounded up in surprise "actions"—by suddenly closing off an area and arresting them or by sending "work" orders. They were then herded into trains or trucks, and brought to the death camps.

Every step of the way, the Nazis treated the Jews with cruelty and abuse. When the Jews were being rounded up, they would be hit, humiliated, and attacked by dogs. Then they would be crammed into cattle cars—sometimes up to a thousand people in a closed car without windows—and taken on journeys, which would last for days, to the concentration camps. In the camps they suffered further terrible acts of cruelty.

The death camps were described

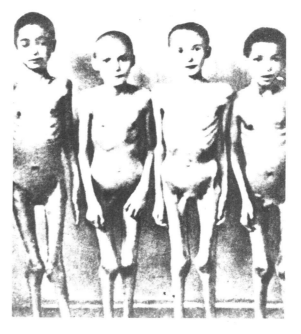

as "another planet." The inmate was stripped of his identity, his name, his family and friends. Human life had no value. Cruel guards tortured the inmates and watched their every step. Starvation turned people into the living dead. They were forced to work until they dropped. "Medical experiments" were carried out on the inmates of several camps. Joseph Mengele, an S.S. doctor at

The Danes actively resisted the Nazi attempts to carry out the "Final Solution" in their country by evacuating all the Jews in Denmark to Sweden in fishing boats, as shown above.

Above left: The death camps were described by their inmates as "another planet." In April 1945, the French artist P.C. Dabouis painted the inmates of Dachau after the camp had been liberated.

Left: Twins in Joseph Mengele's "experiments."

Top left: Raoul Wallenberg, who was imprisoned by the Russians at the end of the war.

Top right: Jewish children hidden in a Catholic monastery.

Hannah Szenes before leaving on the rescue mission from which she did not return.

A statue of Mordechai Anielewicz in Kibbutz Yad Mordechai, which is named after him.

Auschwitz, was responsible for the death of many Jewish prisoners as a result of his cruel experiments. The crematoria in the extermination camps worked day and night, and even then could not manage to burn all the bodies of those killed in the gas chambers.

The net in which the Jewish people were caught at the time of the Holocaust became even tighter because of the attitude of the local populations. In occupied countries and inside Nazi Germany, most of the people did not care about the fate of the Jewish people, and many even helped the murderers. Only a few, known as Righteous Gentiles, could not accept what was being done. They risked their lives to save Jews. Most of the rescuers felt a deep sense of sympathy for the persecuted Jews. Two Righteous Gentiles deserve special mention for their remarkable deeds: the Consul of Portugal in Bordeaux, France— Aristides De Sousa Mendes—who gave thousands of Jews entry permits to his country in 1940, and the Swedish diplomat Raoul Wallenberg, who saved tens of thousands of Hungarian Jews.

In Denmark, the attitude of the local population was different from the rest of Europe. The Jews of Denmark were untouched by Nazi abuse until 1943, because the Danes insisted that the Germans respect their rights. In the fall of that year, the Danes found out that the Germans planned to apply the "Final Solution" to Denmark's 8,000 Jews.

Different groups immediately began to organize themselves and draw up plans for rescue operations. First, the Jews were warned of what lay in store for them. Then hiding places were prepared. Finally, all the Jews were taken in fishing boats to the shores of neutral Sweden.

In Palestine, many Jews joined the British army. The Jewish community of Palestine was not able to help the Jews of Europe very much. Some attempts were made but these were not successful. One outstanding effort to help the Jews of Europe was made by a small group of Palestinian Jewish parachutists who were dropped into Europe in order to help smuggle Jews out. One of them was the Hungarian-born Hannah Szenes. She was captured in Hungary, tortured, and executed.

As for the free world, it could have exerted pressure on the Nazis. There was much it could have done to stop, at least partially, the slaughter of the Jews. But for the most part it did nothing. The Allied countries which fought Nazi Germany did not see the Holocaust of the European Jews as a problem which needed special action.

JEWISH RESISTANCE

The chance of saving oneself from the German trap by rebelling was nil. The German stranglehold tightening around the Jews did not leave much chance of escape. Rebellion meant choosing death with honor—instead of going like sheep to the slaughter. The poet Abba Kovner, the commanders of the Vilna ghetto underground, said in 1945, referring to those who would survive: "We wanted to remain alive in their memory."

There were many Jewish uprisings during the Holocaust. The more famous ones happened in Warsaw, Bialystok, Kharkov, and Bedzin. The Warsaw ghetto uprising became

a symbol of Jewish resistance against the Nazis. It began on the eve of Passover, 1943. Groups of anti-Nazi fighters formed the "Jewish Fighting Organization." They managed to get hold of weapons and to make bombs in the ghetto. With these bombs they attacked the Germans. The commander of the uprising, Mordechai Anielewicz, wrote to his friend Itzhak Zuckerman, also a resistance commander: "Something way above and beyond our boldest dreams has happened: the Germans have twice retreated from the ghetto. The main thing is that the dream of my life has come true. I have had the fortune to set my eyes upon Jewish defense in the ghetto in all its greatness."

The Germans attacked the ghetto and burned house after house. The fighting continued until May 8, when the command bunker fell. By then, only a few of the 55,000 Jews in the ghetto at the start of the uprising were still alive.

Many Jews also joined groups of partisans, or freedom fighters. In 1943, uprisings even broke out in two of the death camps—Treblinka and Sobibor. Several hundred Jews, who were forced to burn corpses and sort victims' clothing and belongings, succeeded in rebelling and even in escaping from the camp.

There were also uprisings in several work camps. From the outset these uprisings had virtually no chance of success. They expressed, above all, a heroic spirit against all odds.

The Germans still went on with the destruction of the Jews even after Germany began to weaken. In

1941 America entered the war, and in January 1943, Russia defeated the German army on the Stalingrad front. On June 6, 1944 ("D-Day"), the Allied forces landed at Normandy, France, under the command of General Dwight D. Eisenhower, and began to liberate

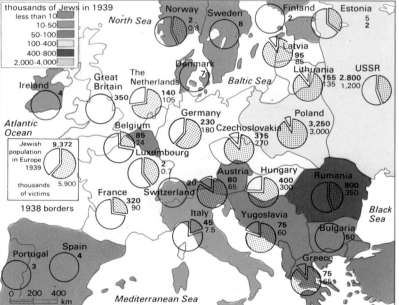

Europe. Russia started to crush the Germans from the east. Hitler committed suicide on April 30, 1945, and on May 4, Germany surrendered.

The war in Europe was over. In the Far East the war continued until August, and ended when the U.S. Air Force dropped the atom bomb on the Japanese cities of Hiroshima and Nagasaki.

About 30 million people were killed in this terrible and cruel war—six million of them Jews, about one-third of the Jewish nation.

In 1939 Europe had approximately 9.4 million Jews. Of those, about six million died in the Holocaust (see map). Key to numbers: in bold type is the number of Jews in 1939, and below that is the number of victims.

87

20

A STATE IN THE MAKING

The Jews in Palestine waged a constant war against the British restrictions on immigration and settlement. But when World War II broke out on September 1, 1939, and Britain began to fight the Nazis, the Jews had to reconsider their own struggle against the British. David Ben-Gurion became the chairman of the Jewish Agency Executive (the executive branch of the World Zionist Organization) in 1935. He stated the Zionist motto: "We shall fight in Eretz Yisrael against the White Paper as if there were no world war, and we shall fight Hitler as if there were no White Paper." The White Paper was the British document in which the limitation on Jewish immigration and settlement was published. By cooperating with the British, the Jews hoped to help defeat the Nazis and to defend Eretz Yisrael.

The battlefront in World War II came close to Palestine's northern and southern borders. Syria and Lebanon in the north were ruled by

The diagram below shows how important industry in Palestine was to the British during World War II.

"But do you have a certificate?" (a permit to enter Palestine), the British officer asks the drowning illegal immigrant, in a cartoon from 1939.

WORLD WAR II IN ERETZ YISRAEL

The Jewish community in Palestine joined in the war effort. About 100,000 foreign soldiers were stationed in the country, and they needed goods and services which were supplied by the local factories. The farmers also planted new crops to help feed these soldiers.

But despite this cooperation, the British did not change their policy toward the Jewish community in Palestine. When the war began, they banned Jews from Nazi-controlled areas of Europe from entering the country. The purpose of this order was to prevent spies from infiltrating Palestine, but it made it very difficult to rescue the Jews who managed to escape from the Nazis. Those who were caught by the British as they tried to reach Eretz Yisrael were put back to sea or held in detention camps. Several ships sank trying to get to Palestine or after the British had turned them back. One of these was the ship *Struma,* which sank in the Black Sea

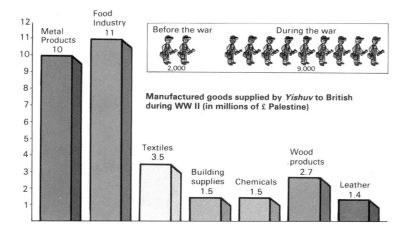

Before the war — 2,000 / During the war — 9,000

Manufactured goods supplied by *Yishuv* to British during WW II (in millions of £ Palestine)

Metal Products 10 — Food Industry 11 — Textiles 3.5 — Building supplies 1.5 — Chemicals 1.5 — Wood products 2.7 — Leather 1.4

Vichy France, and the French government at that time supported the Nazis. In the south German troops were advancing on Egypt.

in February 1942, with 800 Jewish refugees on board. But a few small ships still managed to smuggle 15,000 illegal immigrants from Europe into Palestine during the war. Starting in 1942, illegal immigrants were also brought into the country by land, across the northern border. About 12,000 Jews from Muslim countries reached Eretz Yisrael in this way.

The British still tried to keep the immigrants from coming in, and often searched the Jewish settlements, looking for illegal immigrants and weapons.

The Jewish National Fund also continued to buy as much land as possible in Palestine. They managed to purchase hundreds of acres, about 80 percent in areas where the Jews were actually forbidden to buy land. In 1939–1940, fifteen new stockade and tower settlements were built, and in 1941-1945, 37 new settlements were established.

Throughout 1942, information had reached Eretz Yisrael about the murder of the Jews in Europe. In the fall of that year, the Jewish leaders in the country began to understand the full meaning of the Holocaust and the "Final Solution" of the Nazis who wanted to exterminate all of the Jews. The Jewish Agency

At first the British did not send them to Europe as they had hoped. But finally, after constant argument and pressure on the British, a Jewish Brigade was formed and sent to fight in Italy. Jewish parachutists were dropped into Nazi-controlled areas of Europe to gather information for the British Army and to make contact with the partisans and the Jewish underground fighters there.

THE HEBREW MOVEMENT OF THE REVOLT

There was a change in government in England after the war. Many people hoped that there would also be a change of policy toward the Jews in Palestine. It was now also clear just what the Nazis had done. Six million Jews had died in the Holocaust, and those who survived had no homes to go back to. But the new British Labor government, and especially the foreign minister Ernest Bevin, decided aginst ease the limitations on Jewish immigration and settlement. As British soldiers were no longer fighting a war, their government sent them to Palestine to prevent the survivors of the Holocaust from entering the country. The entire Jewish

In the above poster: Sir Harold MacMichael, the British high commissioner in Palestine, was accused of the sinking of the ship Struma.

Far left below: British soldiers searched for weapons in Kibbutz Ramat Ha-Kovesh in November 1943. Buildings were destroyed, and shots were fired.

About 4,800 Jewish women from Palestine volunteered for the British army, below center. They served as drivers, clerks, and nurses.

organized a Relief Committee to help the Jews escaping from Europe.

In order to fight the Nazis, 30,000 Jewish men and women in Palestine volunteered for the British Army.

community now realized, as newspaper headlines declared, that "the war is over, but our war continues," and they joined in the struggle against Britain. There were several Jewish military organizations

Refugees, still wearing their yellow badges, arrive in Palestine in 1944. They were caught by the British and placed in detention camps.

89

Lehi blew up a railway track after two of its members, who were arrested by the British, blew themselves up before they could be executed.

Illegal Jewish immigrants who came on refugee boats, far right, were taken ashore at night.

Jewish refugees, shown at right, were smuggled across the snow-covered mountains of Europe to ports on the Mediterranean Sea, where they boarded ships for Eretz Yisrael.

held in a detention camp were released by force. Later there were attacks on British radar stations used to detect immigrant ships, on British Coast Guard boats, and on airfields.

in Palestine: the Haganah ("defense"), the major security force of the Jewish community; the Palmach, whose name was derived from the first letters of "Attack Companies," which was a part of the Haganah; the Izl (pronounced "etzel"), from the first letters of National Military Organization, an underground organization that supported constant armed resistance to the British; and Lehi, Fighters for the Freedom of Israel, another underground organization. They all cooperated in the battle against the British, and the joint forces were called the Hebrew Movement of the Revolt. The first action took place on October 10, 1945. The illegal immigrants who were being

The British responded with constant searches and arrests. The worst day for the Jewish community was Saturday, June 29, 1946—"Black Saturday"—when about 2,700 Jewish leaders and fighters were arrested.

The Jewish organizations argued among themselves about how to fight the British. Some were in favor of armed attacks, and others preferred resistance and a political struggle. In July 1946, the IZL blew up a wing of the King David Hotel in Jerusalem where the British had their government offices. This violent action shocked many people, and the Haganah decided to stop the activities of the Movement of the Revolt.

But the struggle for immigration and settlement continued. In Europe, the escape organization was formed to care for the Jewish refugees who were left without homes after the Holocaust and to arrange to bring them to Eretz Yisrael. It was very difficult and dangerous work. First the boats had to reach the shore without being discovered by British patrols. If the British were in the area, hundreds of people from nearby settlements would come to the shore and mix with the illegal immigrants. That way the British could not identify them, so naturally they could not arrest them. The immigrants were then taken to the settlements to begin their new life.

The British did everything they

could to stop this illegal Jewish immigration. They put pressure on Italy not to let the immigrant ships leave Italian ports. British warships and planes followed the ships and from mid-August 1947, and until the British left Palestine, almost every ship was captured. The refugees aboard were taken to detention camps in Cyprus. One incident in particular became very famous. On July 11, 1947, the refugee ship *Exodus*

1947 left France with 4,500 illegal immigrants. On July 18 it was caught. The Jewish refugees aboard fought back, but the British were stronger. The ship was brought to the port at Haifa and the immigrants were sent back to Europe by prison ship. The refugees refused to leave the ship in France. They were sent to Hamburg and returned to the camps for displaced people in Germany. Newspapers throughout the world printed the story of the *Exodus,* and many people now learned of the sad fate of these refugees and of their desire to live in

Eretz Yisrael.

Despite constant British attempts to stop immigration, 70,000 refugees from Europe managed to enter the country in 64 ships between May 1945, and late 1947. It was in 1947 that the Jewish community worked especially hard to win political support and to gain the sympathy of people all over the world. The United Nations was now going to debate the future of Eretz Yisrael.

Jewish refugees declared a hunger strike in La Spezia, Italy, when their ship was not allowed to sail for Eretz Yisrael, far left.

The British held 50,000 Jewish refugees in detention camps in Cyprus, left.

The illegal immigrant ship Exodus 1947, above left, after the battle with the British near the coast of Haifa.

21

ESTABLISHING THE STATE OF ISRAEL

Joyous crowds poured into the streets of all the Jewish cities in Palestine, right, after the results of the U.N. vote were broadcast over the radio on the night of November 29, 1947.

A special session of the United Nations General Assembly was opened in New York on April 28, 1947. It met to discuss the future of Palestine. The Russian delegate, Andrei Gromyko, surprised everyone by stating that his country supported the Jewish demands for a state of their own. The Arab governments declared that they would oppose such a state by force. On November 29, 1947, the General Assembly decided—with a majority of 33 in favor, 13 against, 10 abstaining, and one absent—to divide Palestine into two states—one Jewish and one Arab. The Jews in Eretz Yisrael were ecstatic, and thousands of people filled the streets, singing and dancing. The Arabs immediately showed what they thought of the U.N. decision. On that very day, a Jewish bus on its way to Jerusalem was attacked. The

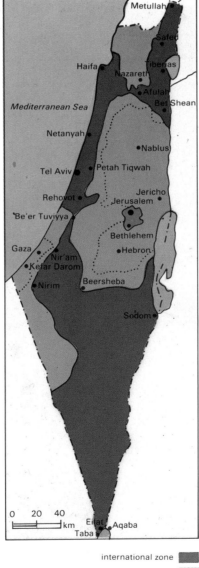

For	Against
Australia	Afghanistan
Belgium	Cuba
Bolivia	Egypt
Brazil	Greece
Byelorussian SSR	India
Canada	Iran
Costa Rica	Iraq
Czechoslovakia	Lebanon
Denmark	Pakistan
Dominican Republic	Saudi Arabia
Ecuador	Syria
France	Turkey
Guatemala	Yemen
Haiti	
Iceland	**Abstain**
Liberia	Argentina
Luxemburg	Chile
Netherlands	China
New Zealand	Colombia
Nicaragua	El Salvador
Norway	Ethiopia
Panama	Honduras
Paraguay	Mexico
Peru	United Kingdom
Philippines	Yugoslavia
Poland	
Sweden	**Absent**
Ukrainian SSR	Siam
Union of South Africa	
USA	
USSR	
Uruguay	
Venezuela	

The list above shows how the countries voted in the U.N. on November 29, 1947.

The Partition Plan approved by the U.N. on November 29, 1947, is represented in this map. It divided Palestine into two states.

Metullah
Safed
Haifa
Nazareth
Tiberias
Afulah
Bet Shean
Mediterranean Sea
Netanyah
Nablus
Tel Aviv
Petah Tiqwah
Rehovot
Jericho
Jerusalem
Be'er Tuviyya
Bethlehem
Gaza
Hebron
Nir'am
Kefar Darom
Nirim
Beersheba
Sodom

0 20 40
km
Eilat Aqaba
Taba

international zone
proposed Arab state
proposed Jewish state
international border —·—·—
armistice line 1949 ··········

next day, the Arab High Committee declared a general strike. None of the Arabs in Palestine reported for work. The War of Independence had begun.

THE WAR OF INDEPENDENCE

The first part of the war lasted until the British Mandate ended on May 15, 1948. During these months, the Jewish population was attacked by disorganized groups of Arab fighters. There were around one million Arabs in Palestine at the time, and only 600,000 Jews, but the Arabs had no central military organization. About 60,000 Jewish men and women were members of the Jewish fighting organizations, the Haganah, Izl, and Lehi.

Great Britain announced that it would not cooperate in ensuring that the U.N. decision was carried out. It claimed to have a neutral policy, not favoring either side. But in their day-to-day operations the British actually aided the Arabs. For example, they pretended not to notice that soldiers from neighboring Arab countries were

entering Palestine to help fight the Jews.

The Arabs attacked mainly isolated communities, the cities (where both Jews and Arabs lived), and the roads. The Jewish forces fought hardest to keep all the roads open, especially the ones that ran through Arab villages or areas under Arab control. The most important struggle was to keep the road to Jerusalem open. Jerusalem's Jews depended for their survival on supplies brought in from the coastal plain. The narrow road to the city ran between high hills on either side. The Arabs controlled these hills and fired on any Jewish vehicles that tried to reach Jerusalem. The trucks moved in convoys—several trucks driving one behind the other— carrying supplies and soldiers. Before the British left Palestine, these soldiers had to hide their weapons because British police often stopped the convoys and took away whatever guns they found. Only a few trucks were armor-plated to protect the men and women inside. As the "War for the Roads" progressed, special armored buses

called "sandwich" buses were built. Still, many Jews were killed trying to get supplies through to Jerusalem.

At the end of March 1948, the Arabs were very close to achieving one of their major aims—cutting the Jewish territory up into areas isolated from each other. The Jewish section of Jerusalem, with 100,000 residents, was cut off from the rest of the country. Food and water in

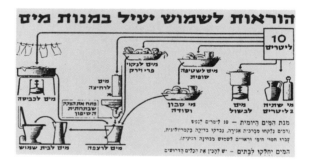

the city had to be rationed.

The turning point came with the Haganah's Operation Nachshon on April 3–5, 1948, when the Jewish fighters managed to capture key points along the road to Jerusalem. In this operation, weapons from Czechoslovakia were used for the first time. The Jewish organizations also bought other weapons but the British did not allow them into the country.

As the time came for the end of the British Mandate, it was necessary to prepare the government institutions that the future Jewish state would need. In April 1948, the National Council was established. Thirteen of its thirty-seven members were then selected to form the National Executive. They quickly set up the government services of justice, police, post, taxes,

Below: On May 14, 1948, standing under a picture of Theodor Herzl, David Ben-Gurion declared the establishment of the State of Israel.

The British searched for weapons in the convoys bringing supplies to Jerusalem, above far left.

The Arabs attacked the armored "sandwich" buses trying to get through to Jerusalem, above center.

When water was rationed in Jerusalem, the instructions shown at center were published. Each person received ten liters (about two and a half gallons) of water a day—two for cooking, one for drinking, and the rest for washing clothes, food, and dishes. This water was then collected in a bucket to be used for washing floors.

The map of the cease-fire borders of Israel in 1949.

The photograph below shows the flag decorated spontaneously in ink and raised in Eilat at the end of a military operation in which Israeli soldiers reached the southern border of the country.

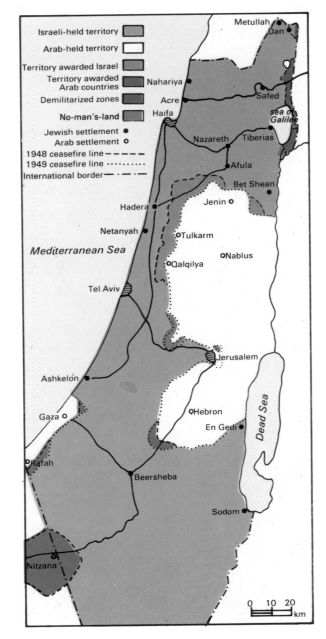

When the British left the police station building in the Galilee in April 1948, shown at right, it was taken over by the Arabs who thus controlled the road below. Today, it is called Fort Koah, named for the 28 fighters who died in the battle to capture it. (Koah means "strength" in Hebrew, but also has the numerical value of 28.)

A transit camp for new immigrants in the Galilee, right.

sanitation, and welfare.

On the afternoon of Friday, May 14, 1948, in the Tel Aviv Museum, David Ben-Gurion declared the establishment of the State of Israel.

The next day, on May 15, the last British soldier left Eretz Yisrael and the United States recognized the new state. The Soviet Union announced its recognition of Israel two days later. In response, armies from all the neighboring Arab countries then attacked Israel, and the full-scale war for Israel's independence really began.

Until then, the Israeli soldiers had been fighting in the underground. They now faced well-trained and well-equipped Arab forces. It was only the amazing courage and devotion of the Israeli fighters that

kept the Arabs from defeating the new state immediately.

More weapons began to arrive in Israel, and after only ten days of fighting, the newly created Israeli army, the Israel Defense Forces (I.D.F.), launched five major counterattacks, one of which was aimed at gaining total control of the road to Jerusalem. The Arab forces were surprised by the I.D.F.'s attacks. They agreed to a 28-day truce, called by the U.N., to begin on June 11. Israel used the truce to refresh and equip its troops.

As soon as the truce ended, fighting began again. During the next ten days, the I.D.F. held its ground around Jerusalem and captured the Arab towns of Lydda, Ramlah, and Nazareth. A second truce, called by a U.N. Security Council Resolution, began on July 18.

This truce, too, was followed by more fighting. The Israeli forces captured the Negev in the south of the country and the Galilee in the north. The Arab countries were now ready to negotiate. The first was Egypt. A cease-fire agreement was

signed in Rhodes on February 24, 1949, between Israel and Egypt. This then served as a model for the agreements with Lebanon, signed on March 23, 1949; with Jordan, signed on April 3; and with Syria, signed on July 20.

The cease-fire was supposed to be the first step toward peace negotiations, but the Arabs would not agree to talk with Israel about peace. The cease-fire borders, where the armies had stopped fighting when the agreements were signed, therefore remained the borders of the State of Israel until the Six-Day War in 1967. The Israelis then began to build their new state.

camps were set up near the cities throughout the country. Their small buildings were first built from canvas and later from corrugated metal. In 1952 these camps housed about 250,000 new immigrants. Most of them spent at least two or three years there until they moved to permanent homes. The last camps were torn down in the 1960s. By the late 1950s, 90 percent of the population of Israel was Jewish.

The many new immigrants needed work. The government provided jobs building roads and planting trees, until the establishment of new settlements and new industries began and there were enough jobs for

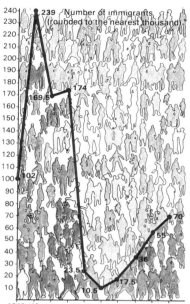

BUILDING AND GROWTH

The first challenge for the new state was immigration. Thousands of Jews now came to Israel. In just three years, from 1948 to 1951, 700,000 immigrants reached the country, more than the entire population of Israel when the state was declared. Survivors of the Holocaust came from the camps for displaced people in Germany and from the British detention camps on Cyprus, as well as from Poland, Rumania, and Bulgaria. From the East, Jews arrived from Yemen, Iraq, Morocco, Algeria, Tunisia, Libya, Turkey, and Afghanistan.

Israel welcomed every Jew, even those who were destitute. With the aid of the Jewish Agency, they were all given basic necessities and a place to live. About one hundred transit

everyone.

In order to expand the areas for farming, water had to be brought to the desert in the south. In July, 1955, the national water carrier was opened. This network of pipes brought water from the Yarkon River sources near Tel Aviv to the Negev in the south. Industry was also developed. New roads were paved and a new port was opened near Haifa. New power plants were built and electric lines laid. During the first ten years of the state, the Israeli Merchant Marine expanded and *El Al* ("Skyward") Israel Airlines was founded. But although the country was growing rapidly, Israel still lived under the shadow of the refusal of the Arab states to live in peace with their new Jewish neighbor.

Between 1948 and 1957, about 900,000 immigrants reached Israel; see chart above. Around 700,000 of them came between 1948 and 1951.

Many new Jewish immigrant settlements were founded in the early years of the state. In the cartoon at left, the Prophet Elijah has trouble finding his way around the rapidly growing young country on the eve of Passover, 1951.

The land in the photograph above was at one time a huge swamp. By 1959 it was drained and could be used for farming.

95

22

The Sinai Campaign and the Six-Day War

Below left: A narrow street in a Arab refugee camp in the Gaza strip.

Israel's geographical position in the heart of the Arab world interfered with Gamal Abdul Nasser's desire to unite the Arab states. In this Egyptian propaganda poster at center below, all of the Arab countries are stabbing bayonets into the "Zionist snake."

France was the first major country to supply Israel with a large quantity of modern weapons. Right: a French-made Mystere jet in the Israel Air Force.

The major I.D.F. forces to fight in the Sinai Campaign were the armored divisions. Below right: Sherman tanks, based upon the model used in World War II, advance in the Sinai Peninsula.

The cease-fire agreements signed with the Arab countries in 1949 did not bring the peace between Israel and its neighbors that everyone in Israel had hoped for. Tens of thousands of Arabs had fled from their homes in Israel during the War of Independence. Israel allowed about 40,000 of these refugees to return in order to be reunited with their families, but declared that the problem as a whole could be discussed only as part of peace negotiations. But still the Arab states refused to sit down and talk peace with Israel. The Arab refugees lived in camps built for them by the U.N. Relief and Works Agency (UNRWA). Bands of terrorists organized in these camps and attacked Israeli targets by night.

The Sinai Campaign

In 1954, Colonel Gamal Abdul Nasser and officers of the Egyptian army overthrew King Farouk of Egypt. Nasser became the president of Egypt. It was his dream to be the leader of the entire Arab world. He tried to unite all of the Arabs with his call for a struggle against "Western imperialism" and especially against Israel. In 1955, Nasser signed an arms deal with Czechoslovakia, which supplied Egypt with hundreds of airplanes, tanks, armored cars, heavy artillery, and warships. Egypt was now a major military force. In July 1956, the Egyptian government took over control of the Suez Canal, which links the Mediterranean with the Far East. The Canal was very important to Britain and France. They began to plan a military operation to capture the Canal and bring down Nasser's government. At the same

time, Israel was afraid that Egypt was going to attack. It was also suffering from constant terrorism and from Egypt's shipping blockade, which extended from the Israeli port of Eilat through the Red Sea.

So Israel joined with Britain and France in their plans against Egypt. The Sinai Campaign began on Monday, October 29, 1956. One hundred hours later, all of the Sinai Peninsula was in the hands of the Israel Defense Forces (I.D.F.), and British and French troops controlled sections of the Suez Canal. The United States and the Soviet Union immediately called for all sides to retreat. Israel withdrew from Sinai after the United States guaranteed freedom of navigation for all ships in the Red Sea.

As a result of the Sinai Campaign, the involvement of the Soviet Union in the Middle East increased, and Nasser's government—and his hatred of Israel—became stronger.

The Six-Day War

Nasser called Israel's withdrawal from Sinai a great victory for Egypt. He remained loyal to his goal of attacking Israel and leading the Arab world. In 1958, Syria and Egypt agreed to unite into one country— the United Arab Republic—under Nasser. Yemen joined them, and

Nasser's representatives in Lebanon and Jordan worked to convince these countries to become part of the U.A.R. as well. The Soviet Union, meanwhile, was supplying Egypt and Syria with a large quantity of weapons, and so the United States provided Israel with new weapons; these were in addition to the airplanes Israel had bought from France and the arms it produced itself.

In 1964, a conference of the Arab leaders in Cairo decided to divert the waters of two sources of the Jordan River in Syria and Lebanon, so that Israel's National Water Carrier would not have enough water. At this time, the terrorist organizations, the Palestine Liberation Organization (P.L.O.) and the Palestine Liberation Movement (Fatah), were also established. Fatah's first terrorist action was to plant a bomb in a section of the National Water Carrier. Other actions were launched from Jordan and Lebanon. The I.D.F. retaliated against the countries from which the terrorists operated.

On May 15, 1967, Nasser sent his troops into Sinai and closed the passage from the Red Sea to the port of Eilat. U.N. overseers had kept this passage open since the Sinai Campaign, but Nasser simply told them to leave. Nasser knew very well that Israel would have to go to war to keep this vital shipping line open. Then Jordan's King Hussein signed a defense pact with Egypt, which Iraq joined later.

The Israeli government decided to wait and see if the United States would be able to keep the promise it had made after the Sinai Campaign and convince Egypt to let ships through to Eilat. But in the meanwhile, shelters and trenches were prepared in all of Israel's cities and villages, and the I.D.F.'s reserves were put on the alert. The fear of war hung over the country.

The first American weapons supplied directly to Israel were the Hawk anti-aircraft missiles, above left, which arrived in 1962.

Trenches were dug in Tel Aviv in 1967, left, to protect the population from a sudden air attack.

The Yarmuk River near the Israel-Jordan border, shown above, is part of Jordan's irrigation project.

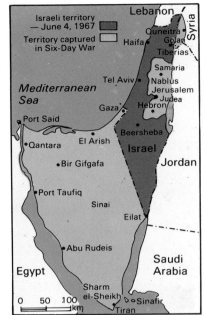

From the Golan Heights, shown above, there is a panoramic view of the Israeli settlements in the Hulah Valley.

In the map: Israel's borders before and after the Six-Day War.

At the start of the Six-Day War, the Israel Air Force bombed Egyptian planes still on the ground, shown above right.

Israeli soldiers stand before the Western Wall—the only remnant of the Temple destroyed in 70 C.E.—after the eastern half of Jerusalem was captured on June 6, 1967.

Within a few days it became clear that the United States could not open Egypt's blockade by diplomacy and would not send its soldiers to break it open. At dawn on June 5, 1967, the Israel Air Force launched a pre-emptive attack on the airfields of Egypt. Ground forces took the Gaza Strip and the Sinai Peninsula, in only four days. Jordan joined in the attack and as the I.D.F. fought back, it captured Judea and Samaria to the west of the Jordan River. Syria shelled the settlements in the north, and in its battles here the I.D.F. conquered the Golan Heights and the southern slopes of Mount Hermon. On June 10, six days after it had begun, the war was over.

The Six-Day War brought about a big change in Israel's security. Three Arab military forces had been defeated, water resources were safeguarded, the dangerous "narrow waist" of the country between Samaria and the sea was broadened, and Jerusalem, Israel's capital since the days of King David, was now reunited with its eastern half, which had been captured from Jordan. In the south Israel now held all of the Sinai Peninsula, to provide a warning against any new attack by Egypt. But above all else, Israel now hoped that its military victory would force the Arab states to make peace.

The Israeli government declared that it would withdraw from most of the conquered territory in exchange for peace. But immediately after the war, the

heads of the Arab countries met in Khartoum, Sudan, and agreed on a policy known as the "three no's": no recognition of Israel, no negotiations with Israel, and no peace.

On November 22, 1967, the U.N. Security Council adopted a compromise—Resolution 242. It called for a just and lasting peace in the Middle East. The I.D.F. would withdraw from the conquered territories and there would be an end to the war. All the countries in the region would respect the right of their neighbors to live in peace within secure and recognized borders. Freedom of navigation on the international waterways would be guaranteed, and there would be a just solution to the refugee problem. However, the U.N. did not have any real power to carry out Resolution 242.

ISRAEL'S DEVELOPMENT

The two wars in 1956 and 1967 did not slow the rapid development of Israel. There were now fewer immigrants, and fewer new settlements were established, but several important projects were completed during these years. A new port was opened in Ashdod, phosphate mining and processing plants were built near the Dead Sea, and the port of Eilat was expanded. The most important project was the completion of the National Water Carrier, which brought water from the Sea of Galilee in the north to the Negev desert in the south. In December 1960, Israel announced

the construction, with French assistance, of a large nuclear reactor in Dimona, and in July 1963 it joined the Moscow Accord which banned nuclear testing in the atmosphere.

The standard of living in the country rose rapidly, and imports increased to such an extent that Israel had a serious deficit in its balance of payments, which means that it spent more money than it earned from exports. So, at the end of 1966, the government decided to reduce its spending, and many people who worked in government jobs found themselves unemployed just before the outbreak of the Six-Day War. The gap between the comfortable veteran settlers and many of the poorer new immigrants, especially those from Islamic countries, grew larger. Several violent demonstrations broke out because of this.

After the speedy victory in the Six-Day War—which surprised the Israelis as much as the Arabs—the economy of Israel began to improve. The country returned to a state of

full employment, even providing jobs for thousands of workers from the administered territories captured in the war. The construction industry began to boom. New neighborhoods were built in Jerusalem, and Tel Aviv expanded until fully half of the population of Israel made its home there. The country was enjoying its prosperity, but was concerned about the presence of about one million Arabs now living in the administered territories, with around 270,000 in refugee camps.

Within Israel, people debated the future of the territories. Some felt that they should officially be made part of the country, both because of the Jewish people's historical ties to these lands, and because of Israel's security needs. Others believed that the one million Arab inhabitants were a threat to the Jewish

New neighborhoods, shown top left, were built in East Jerusalem after the Six-Day War.

The National Water Carrier, top right, began operation in the summer of 1965.

After the Six-Day War, the bridges over the Jordan River were rebuilt. Since then people and goods have passed over them between Israel and Jordan. Shown in the picture at left above: some of the people from Judea and Samaria, who fled to Jordan during the war, return to their homes.

The Port of Ashdod in the center of Israel, above.

99

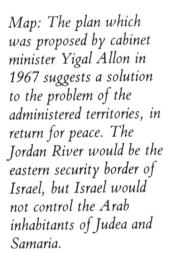

character of Israel and the territories should be returned, with or without peace. The third position, held by most of the government ministers, was that Israel should continue to hold the territories until the Arabs agreed to peace. But everyone agreed that Israel would never allow the situation to return to what it had been before the Six-Day War—that of insecure borders and the constant threat of war. The government decided to establish settlements in the territories in places that would help ensure the security of the country.

Although the Six-Day War had ended in a cease-fire, Israel was still not free from attack. The Egyptians shelled the Sinai Peninsula, trying to make the I.D.F. move back from the Suez Canal. The P.L.O. set up bases in Jordan from which they launched terrorist actions and shelled Israeli settlements in the Beit Shean and Jordan Valleys. The terrorists then

threatened to overthrow King Hussein of Jordan. In September 1970 (called "Black September" by the P.L.O.), the king ordered an attack upon the terrorists and had them thrown out of his country. Although Syria supported the terrorist organizations, it too would not allow them to operate from its territory. So the P.L.O. moved its centers to Lebanon. It set up its headquarters in Beirut and took over total control of South Lebanon, a region that became known as "Fatah-land." From there, they set out on terrorist raids in Israel and shelled the northern Israeli settlements, as well as planning attacks on Israeli targets in Europe, such as embassies and El Al airport facilities. Israel responded by hitting their camps and headquarters. For a while it seemed that Israel's greatest security problem was now the war against the terrorists.

23
THE KIBBUTZ

The kibbutz movement is one of Zionism's most innovative creations. It began when the first Zionists settled in the Land of Israel at the beginning of the 20th century. The kibbutz provided a way for these pioneers to build the country and redeem the land.

The first kibbutz was established in 1909 at Umm Juni by the Sea of Galilee when ten young men and two young women started a small farming operation. The work was very difficult and the conditions very harsh. They simply could not do it alone. So they decided to work and live together, basing their community on cooperation and mutual aid. This was the beginning of the first communal settlement—Deganyah. In Hebrew the word *kibbutz* means group, grouping, gathering together.

A New Society

The kibbutz movement is a part of the Histadrut General Federation of Labor. The ideology of the *kibbutzim* is both Zionistic and socialistic. Its aim was originally to bring about a national revolution, through immigration to and settlement in Eretz Yisrael. Life in the kibbutz is based on the ideals of cooperation, equality, mutual aid, work, and a free and democratic society.

In the years of the British Mandate, before the establishment of the State of Israel, when the Jewish community was fighting for its independence, kibbutzim served as Haganah bases. They were also the home base for the people sent abroad to educate Jewish youth and organize illegal immigration. The kibbutzim were often the first new home for the illegal immigrants. Because they were scattered throughout the country, the kibbutzim helped to determine Israel's borders, and made it possible for Jews to live in all parts of the country.

Today in 1987, more than 130,000 people live on 270 kibbutzim throughout Israel. Some of the newer ones are small, with only a

At left below: Decisions on a kibbutz are made by a general meeting of all the members.

Kibbutz Ein Harod in the Jezreel Valley was founded in 1921. Shown at bottom left, members participating in an agricultural festival, celebrating one of their first harvests.

Kibbutz Farod in the Upper Galilee, below, was founded in 1949 by a group of youngsters from Hungary who came to Israel after World War II.

Top: The kibbutz clothing store supplies clothes for all the community's adults and children.

A group of first-graders in a kibbutz school, above center.

Kibbutz members developed original ways of celebrating the holidays which combine traditional Jewish values with typically Israeli elements. In the photograph above right, Kibbutz Maoz Hayim in Beit Shean Valley celebrates the beginning of the harvest. The ceremony, held during Passover, is the modern version of the Biblical custom of bringing the first crops to the Temple in Jerusalem.

The Granot regional factory, shown above, processes agricultural produce. It is owned collectively by several kibbutzim.

few dozen members. Others are very large, with over one thousand people whose ages span four generations.

Kibbutz membership is voluntary. It is a democratic society in which decisions are made by a general meeting of all its members. Committees are responsible for carrying out these decisions in areas such as work, culture, and finance. The activities of the committees are coordinated by the secretary, treasurer, and work programmer. The members take turns filling these jobs.

Communal consumption, production, and ownership are basic principles of the kibbutz. This means that everything is owned by all of the members together, and the kibbutz is responsible for supplying the needs of each of them. This is done through institutions like the central dining hall, the clothing store, and the grocery and general store where each member can choose what he needs and likes, using the budget he is given.

Another principle of the kibbutz is communal education. The child belongs to a group made up of children his own age and is cared for by members chosen for this job. He spends most of his time with this group, except for the afternoon hours, Saturdays, and holidays which he spends with his family. In recent years, many kibbutzim have arranged for the young children to sleep at home instead of in the communal children's houses. Most

kibbutzim have their own local elementary school, while most secondary schools are regional. Kibbutz schools also accept children from outside the kibbutz.

Culture is very important to the kibbutz, and many artists live and work on kibbutzim. The kibbutz movement has dance groups, orchestras, choirs, a theater, and two publishing houses. Many kibbutzim also have their own art galleries or museums.

THE KIBBUTZ ECONOMY

The kibbutzim were all originally farming communities. They are involved in all branches of agriculture, which today is highly modernized. Over the past years, the kibbutzim have also begun to work in the services and industry, and today every kibbutz has at least one factory, in addition to its fields, orchards, and livestock. Kibbutz industries produce 6.5% of the industrial output of Israel. Although only 3.5% of Israel's Jewish population live on kibbutzim, their contribution to the national economy in agricultural and industrial production and export is proportionally much higher.

People in Israel and around the world see the kibbutz as a unique social experiment; scholars study its structure and way of life. Many years ago, the Jewish philosopher Martin Buber defined the kibbutz as "a distinct non-failure." After eighty years, many people would now define it as a distinct success.

24

ROADS TO PEACE

After thirty years, Israel was finally able to sign a peace agreement with its southern neighbor, Egypt. But this was only after the country had suffered another painful war—the Yom Kippur War of October 1973.

THE YOM KIPPUR WAR

Despite the defeat of the Arab countries in the Six-Day War, their goal remained the same—to wipe the State of Israel off the map. The Soviet Union continued to supply Syria and Egypt with weapons, until their military strength became greater than Israel's.

In 1970, President Nasser of Egypt died, and Anwar Sadat became the new Egyptian president. Sadat wanted to "break the [Egyptian] barrier of fear" of Israel, as he called it. But in order to defeat Israel on the battlefield, he would have to take the country by surprise.

On Yom Kippur, October 6, 1973, the armies of Egypt and Syria attacked. Yom Kippur, the Day of Atonement, is the holiest day in the Jewish calendar. It is a day of fasting, and is the only day of the year when transportation, both public and private, stops completely in Israel. The radio and television stations do not broadcast, and many

of Israel's citizens spend the entire day at prayer in the synagogues. Thousands of soldiers were driven directly to the front from the synagogues.

During the first days of the war, many Israeli soldiers were killed or taken prisoner on both the Egyptian and Syrian fronts. Then, on October 14, the I.D.F. stopped a new Egyptian armored attack. On the night of October 15-16, I.D.F. tank and paratroop forces crossed the Suez Canal into Egypt. Within a few days, Israeli soldiers were only 101 km (63 miles) from the Egyptian

This pontoon bridge over the Suez Canal, shown at far left, was one of three bridges over which the I.D.F. crossed the Suez Canal into Egypt during the Yom Kippur War.

Children held hostage by terrorists in the northern Israeli town of Ma'alot are rescued by I.D.F. soldiers, left.

Below: The Egyptian front in the south—shown on the left—and the Syrian front in the north—shown on the right—during the Yom Kippur War.

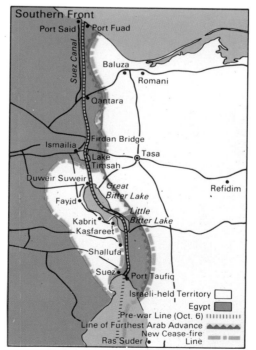

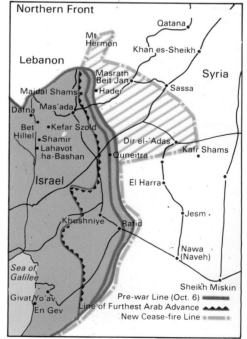

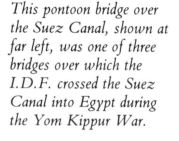

capital of Cairo, and had surrounded Egyptian troops in Sinai.

During the war, the United States airlifted large quantities of arms to Israel. But at the same time, the American secretary of state, Henry Kissinger, was pressuring Israel to sign a cease-fire agreement. In 1974, armistice agreements were signed, and the prisoners of war taken by all sides were returned to their countries.

PEACE WITH EGYPT

After the Yom Kippur War, Sadat apparently realized that the Arab countries could not defeat Israel on the battlefield. He hoped that Israel, in exchange for peace, would agree to withdraw to the borders that had existed before the Six-Day War in 1967. So on November 9, 1977, he declared that he was willing to speak before the Israeli parliament, the Knesset, in order to end the state of war between the two countries. Just ten days later, he flew to Israel and was greeted with wild enthusiasm all along the road to Jerusalem. Sadat proposed the establishment of peaceful relations, and in return he required that Israel

Photo below right: Egyptian President Anwar Sadat (on the left), Prime Minister of Israel Menahem Begin (center), and President Jimmy Carter, during negotiations prior to the signing of the peace agreement.

Below: Lt. Col. Yonatan Netanyahu, who was the commander of the Entebbe rescue operation.

Above: American secretary of state Henry Kissinger helped reach an armistice agreement after the Yom Kippur War. Here Kissinger, on the left, lands in Israel.

withdraw from Sinai and promise to solve the problem of the Palestinian Arabs.

After Sadat's visit to Jerusalem, Israel and Egypt began peace negotiations. The arguments over the details of the agreement went on for a long time. Henry Kissinger worked hard to help the two sides come to an agreement. The other

Arab countries strongly opposed these negotiations. They threw Egypt out of the Arab League and stopped sending economic aid to the country. The various terrorist organizations, obviously, did not agree with Sadat. But Sadat remained firm. He claimed that peace was vital not only for Egypt, but for the entire Middle East.

Since 1974, there had again been a large number of terrorist actions against Israeli targets, both in Israel and in other countries. One of these took place in June 1976. An Air France plane was hijacked on its way from Athens to Israel and forced to land in Entebbe, Uganda. The hijackers demanded that terrorists imprisoned in Israel be freed in return for the release of the passengers and the airplane. In a very bold operation, Israeli planes landed at Entebbe and the hostages were rescued. The commander of the operation, Yonatan Netanyahu, was killed.

Another shocking terrorist action took place in Israel in March 1978. A bus traveling along the highway between Haifa and Tel Aviv was hijacked and thirty-five Israelis were killed. The I.D.F. responded by attacking the terrorist bases in South Lebanon. Shortly afterwards, UNIFIL (U.N. International Force in Lebanon) troops were stationed in the region to help prevent more attacks. But the terrorist actions did not stop, and the shelling of Israeli settlements in the Northern Galilee continued.

With the active participation of the president of the United States, Jimmy Carter, the peace agreement between Israel and Egypt was finally signed at the White House on March 26, 1979. Israel began its preparations for withdrawal from Sinai, which was completed in April 1982, despite the strong objections of the Israeli settlers in the region.

On October 6, 1981, the eighth

anniversary of the start of the Yom Kippur War, President Sadat was murdered in Cairo at a military parade by a group of army officers who were Moslem fanatics and who did not approve of his policies. Nevertheless, his successor, Hosni Mubarak, remained loyal to Sadat's policy of peace with Israel. But near Israel's northern border, the terrorist organizations were growing stronger. On June 6, 1982, the I.D.F. launched an attack in Lebanon to destroy the terrorist bases located in the refugee camps and the city of Beirut, and to force the Syrian soldiers there to leave. Israel hoped that a strong Christian government would take power in Lebanon and would be willing to sign a peace agreement with Israel.

The war in Lebanon, called the Peace for Galilee Operation, went on longer than expected, and although the terrorist camps were badly damaged and many terrorists were forced to leave Lebanon, the terrorist organizations could not be completely destroyed. Many people in Israel were now opposed to the long war, especially when I.D.F. soldiers began to get caught in the crossfire of the fighting between rival groups in Lebanon, a country in which people of many different faiths live.

In fact, during 1983–1984 there were many conflicts within Israel: the gap grew between the more comfortable western Jews and the poorer eastern Jews; between extremist religious Jews, who wanted to make everyone follow the religious laws, and secular Jews; between the left-wing parties, who demanded the immediate withdrawal from Lebanon and an end to the increasing settlement in Judea and Samaria, and the right-wing parties who held the opposite views; between Jewish and Arab citizens of Israel; and even among the Arabs themselves, between those who wanted to live in peace with the Jews, and extreme nationalists who still wanted to destroy Israel.

At the end of 1984, a National Unity Government was formed in Israel and this helped to reduce many of these conflicts. In January 1985, the government decided to remove Israeli forces from Lebanon. The I.D.F. remained only in a narrow security zone near Israel's northern border which it patroled together with a Lebanese force, the South Lebanon Army, and UNIFIL.

WITHIN ISRAEL

In 1987, 4.2 million people lived in Israel (not including the administered territories captured in the Six-Day War). 17% of the

Photo at left below: Egyptian president Hosni Mubarak, left, talks with Yitzhak Navon, Israel's president from 1978 to 1983.

I.D.F. soldiers, below, had to use force to remove some of the settlers in the Sinai town of Yamit when they refused to leave their homes so that the region could be turned over to Egypt after the peace agreement was signed.

Israeli soldiers in a Lebanese village, 1?

Far left: About 45,000 Arabs live in Nazareth, the largest Arab city in Israel, which can be seen in the foreground. The Jewish town of Upper Nazareth, with about 26,000 residents, is in the background.

The nomadic life of the Bedouin tribes (right) changed dramatically during the last twenty years, when they started moving to permanent homes (far right).

This is a typical Arab village in Israel today, below right. The mosque rises in the center and modern greenhouses stand nearby.

Far right: A demonstration of Arab youngsters in the administered territories, protesting against Israeli policy.

population is non-Jewish. Most of these are Muslims, but Christians, Druze, and members of other faiths also live in the country. All religious sects have their own institutions which are responsible for matters of religion and personal status such as marriage. The 65,000 Druze who live in Israel enjoy a close relationship with the other citizens of the country, and many of them serve in the Israeli army.

Since the establishment of the State of Israel, a "quiet revolution" has taken place in the economic, social, and political world of Israel's minorities. Arab society has adopted modern political ideas and new technologies. The Arab farmer now uses modern agricultural techniques and produces more crops.

Industrialization has reached even the smallest villages, and many young people move to the cities to find work. An average of 80% of Israeli Arabs vote in each of the elections for the Knesset— proportionally higher than that of the Israeli population as a

whole—and several members of the Knesset come from the non-Jewish population of the country.

Perhaps the greatest change has been in the life of the Bedouins. In the past, these nomadic tribes moved from place to place with their camels and goats, and lived in tents. Today they are settling in permanent villages.

After the Yom Kippur War and the war in Lebanon, many Israeli Arabs became troubled by questions of loyalty and identity. Extreme nationalistic ideas became popular, especially among the young people, some of whom still want to bring an end to Israel. But many Arabs have declared their desire to achieve a "just and lasting peace." The problem, of course, is that each side defines the word "just" in a different way. In 1987 Egypt was the only Arab country which had a peace agreement with Israel. We can only hope that other Arab countries will also agree to live in peace with their Israeli neighbor.

25

IN THE LAND OF GOLDEN OPPORTUNITY

For more than fifty years, there have been more Jews in the United States than in any other country in the world. Together with their unquestioned loyalty to the United States, this large Jewish community maintains close ties with their fellow Jews in Israel and throughout the world.

ORGANIZING THE COMMUNITY

After World War I, there was a spontaneous surge of community feeling among the Jews in America. Many new national organizations were founded, active in religious life, Jewish education, community service, philanthropy, Zionism, and defense against anti-Semitism; the membership of these and previously established organizations grew rapidly. The *B'nai B'rith* ("Sons of the Covenant") organization, founded in 1843 in New York to advance Jewish and humanitarian principles, soon had lodges in almost every city and town wherever Jews lived, and greatly expanded its communal activities. Its Anti-Defamation League, established in 1913, has always fought against anti-Semitism and discrimination of all kinds, working to safeguard the civil rights of every American minority.

The sense of brotherhood felt by American Jewry for Jews the world over led them, as early as the beginning of the 20th century, to establish organizations such as H.I.A.S. (Hebrew Immigrant Aid Society), founded in 1909, and the "Joint" (American Jewish Joint Distribution Committee), founded in

1914. These organizations, with their large membership, helped Jews in distress wherever they were, and aided them in adjusting to their new homes. During World War II, they worked valiantly to rescue the Jews of Europe, but there was little they could do. The endangered Jews were in Nazi-controlled areas, cut off from contact with the Western countries. But as more and more news of the Holocaust reached the United States, the Jewish leaders in the U.S. increased their political activities to save the Jews of Europe. But, the little they could and did do was not enough.

THE AMERICAN ZIONIST MOVEMENT

The Zionist Movement has been active in the United States since the beginning of this century. American

Below: After the 1905 pogroms in Russia, money was collected for welfare and self-defense. Judah Leib Magnes headed the campaign for funds for Russian Jewry, and his name appears on this receipt for contributions.

Photo at bottom: Jewish immigrants from Russia in the office of H.I.A.S., the Hebrew Immigrant Aid Society.

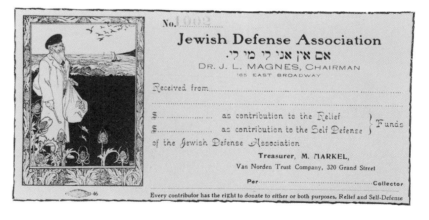

Right: The Blue Box in which donations are collected for the Jewish National Fund.

An advertisement, below, for the United Jewish Appeal, U.S. Jewry's central fundraising organization.

protecting the "little man" against the large companies and property owners. In 1916 he was appointed to the United States Supreme Court. In 1918, Judge Brandeis was elected honorary president of the Zionist Organization of America (Z.O.A.). Albert Einstein (1879–1955), the famous physicist, believed that it was because of his Jewish heritage that he had such a deep love for research, justice, and personal independence. He, too, helped the community in Eretz Yisrael, particularly the Hebrew University. In fact, at one time, he was even nominated to be Israel's first president.

Jewish women have also been active in the Zionist movement.

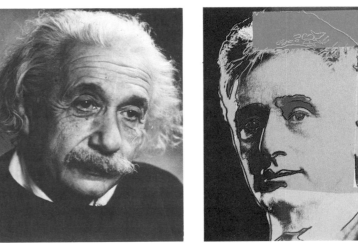

Above right: Hadassah women visiting Jerusalem in 1923.

Above center: Albert Einstein (1879–1955).

The portrait of Judge Louis Dembitz Brandeis, far right, was painted by the famous American artist Andy Warhol (1927–1987).

Jewry, even then, was a source of financial and political support for the Jewish community in Eretz Yisrael. Many Jews who were active in the public life of America also worked to achieve the Zionist aims of establishing a Jewish state in Eretz Yisrael, and to help Jewish communities in other countries. Dr. Judah Leib Magnes (1877–1948), the head of the Zionist Organization of America from 1905–1908, worked to organize the Jewish community of New York before World War I, and later helped found the Hebrew University of Jerusalem in 1925 and was its first president. Justice Louis Brandeis (1856–1941) was one of America's greatest jurists. As a lawyer, he was famous for

Hadassah, the Women's Zionist Organization of America, founded in 1912, devoted itself to the "ideals of Judaism, Zionism and American democracy." Hadassah built a major hospital as well as vocational schools in Israel.

The Holocaust turned many American Jews into strong Zionists. Their position was stated in what is known as the Biltmore Program, named for the hotel in New York City where a conference of Zionist leaders met in May 1942. These leaders demanded that Palestine be opened to Jewish immigration and allowed to become an independent Jewish state. One of the most active leaders of this program was Abba Hillel Silver (1893–1963), a Reform rabbi and the head of the Zionist Emergency Council. He worked hard to convince members of the American government and Congress, as well as United Nations delegates, to support the Zionist demands. And indeed, in 1947, President Harry S. Truman, with

continued to give their financial and political support to the country. The Jewish lobby was founded in 1954 to bring Jewish and Israeli issues to the attention of members of the American Congress. Today the A.I.P.A.C. (American-Israeli Political Action Committee) lobby is

American Jews have held large demonstrations for Jewish causes, such as the march by 1,000 rabbis in 1945, below left, and the protest against British policy in 1947, bottom left.

The photo above shows a parade in honor of Israel's 35th anniversary marching down New York City's Fifth Avenue.

Left: U.S. President Harry S. Truman (on the left), with Abba Eban, the first Israeli ambassador to the United Nations, and David Ben-Gurion (on the right), Israel's first prime minister.

the advice of American Jewish friends, went against the political stream and instructed the U.S. delegate to the United Nations to vote in favor of the plan to divide Palestine between the Arabs and the Jews, to allow the Jews an independent state. He was later the first head of state to recognize Israel.

During the War of Independence some American Jews volunteered to fight in the new-born Israeli army. David Marcus, a graduate of West Point, who served as a colonel in the United States Army in the Second World War, was commander of the Jerusalem front when he was killed.

Since the birth of State of Israel in 1948, the Jews of America have

a model that is envied by other political organizations. American Jewish leaders have convinced many Congressmen that support for Israel is also in the interest of the United States itself, since Israel, like the U.S., is a Western democracy— the only democracy in the Middle East.

AMERICAN JEWRY IN THE 1980S

American Jewry today is highly diverse—religiously, geographically, politically, and in every other respect. By now, Judaism is considered to be America's third significant religious group. Often a rabbi, along with a Protestant clergyman and Catholic priest, is invited to confer a blessing on

109

many official functions, including presidential inaugurations.

Only about 12% of the Jews in the United States today belong to Orthodox Jewry, which carefully observes Jewish religious laws. But there is a resurgence of interest in and commitment to Orthodoxy by young Jews in recent years. Many Jews live in close-knit communities and conscientiously preserve a traditional Jewish way of life. It is believed that a similar number of Jews in America feel no connection at all to Judaism. Most American Jews, however, maintain some ties to their Jewish heritage. About half of them belong to a synagogue, either Reform, Conservative, or Orthodox. These branches of Judaism in America have adopted the idea of the synagogue as a center for cultural and social activities, as well as a place of worship.

Jewish community centers also help to preserve Jewish identity. Initially sponsored by the national Jewish Welfare Board, they were youth clubs which offered the young Jewish immigrants a place for amusement and social activities, and helped them adjust to American society. Many centers today include day-care facilities, halls for concerts, lectures and plays, and athletic and health clubs. At the beginning of the 1980s, there were about 300 Jewish community centers throughout the United States, with about 900,000 members.

Many communities maintain a Jewish Federation and Welfare Fund which is responsible for welfare activities, such as fundraising, hospitals, and aiding the poor and the elderly.

Among the organizations that relate to the United States government are the Presidents' Conference (Conference of Presidents of Major American Jewish Organizations) and the National Jewish Community Relations Advisory Council. These organizations help the community to present one united view to the general public.

Together with their Jewish identity and activities, the Jews in the United States are very much a part of American society. Jews today work in every possible occupation, and many are active in politics.

Right: Rabbi Menachem Schneerson, the leader of Habad Hasidism, in a television appearance.

The Jewish community center in Hillcrest, New York, far right.

A Reform synagogue in New York, below right.

Even non-religious Jews celebrate the major Jewish holidays in order to express their ties to their Jewish heritage. In the photo, below far right, Jewish children dress up as American movie and T.V. heroes on the festival of Purim.

A large percentage of American-born Jews are professionals; many are famous for their participation in the cultural world. Several Jewish authors are considered to be among the important modern American writers, such as Nobel Prize winners Saul Bellow and Isaac Bashevis Singer, as well as Bernard Malamud and Philip Roth. Their books present the experiences of city Jews and Jewish intellectuals.

Jews have also made their mark in the world of entertainment. Shows on Jewish subjects, like *Fiddler on the Roof,* have been Broadway hits. Mel Brooks, Neil Simon, Woody Allen, and other popular Jewish actors and directors, often show their film audiences what it was like for them to grow up Jewish in America.

More than two million Jews, over a third of all the Jews in the United States, still live in and around New York City. However, since the early 1950s, many Jews have left the large cities to live typically American lives in all sections of the country.

Over the years, the Jewish community in the United States has been getting smaller. In the 1980s, there are now—statistically speaking—fewer than two children in the Jewish family, and the number of intermarriages is increasing. This situation raises some questions about the future of American Jewry, in terms of numbers. But the strength of the community rests in the quality of its elite, who continue to make political, social, scientific, and cultural contributions to American society.

Below far left: Woody Allen, the actor and director, in a scene from his movie Annie Hall.

The photo below bottom left shows an American car with HASID as a license plate. It reflects the connection between Judaism and Americanism.

The painting in the center, is by the Jewish artist Mark Rothko (1903–1970), one of the major painters of the abstract style attributed to the group known as the New York School.

Saul Bellow, the American Jewish writer, below.

26

JEWS IN THE EASTERN BLOC

After World War II, the Soviet Union took over the countries of Eastern Europe. This brought the number of Jews living under Soviet rule to three million. Since then the number has dwindled, and more then a million Jews have either emigrated to the west, or have assimilated and have stopped being Jewish.

CHANGING ATTITUDES OF THE SOVIET UNION

During World War II, a movement called the Jewish Anti-Fascist Committee was set up by the Soviet rulers. It was used to encourage Jews to join the anti-Nazi war effort, and also to win support from the Jews of the western world. In 1947 the Soviet Union surprised the world by voting in favor of the establishment of the State of Israel. In return, the Soviets expected Israel to take sides with the Eastern Bloc—against the West in the Middle East. This was met with great enthusiasm by the Jews in the Soviet Union.

At this point, the Soviet government changed its attitude toward the Jews in the Soviet Union. It broke up the Jewish Anti-Fascist Committee and began a bitter propaganda attack against the Jews, Zionism, and the State of Israel. During the rule of the Soviet leader Joseph Stalin (1879–1953), the persecutions increased. Many of the leaders of Soviet Jewry were imprisoned and even executed, among them philosophers, writers, and actors. One leading member of the Jewish community was the actor Shlomo Mikhoels. Though he was supposedly killed in a car accident in 1948, it was obvious that he was murdered on Stalin's orders. Mikhoels was chairman of the Jewish Anti-Fascist Committe, director of the Jewish State Theater in Moscow, and had been awarded the title "People's Actor," the Lenin Decoration, and the Stalin Prize.

Jewish culture came to a standstill, and the Jews of the Soviet Union were cut off from the rest of the world. After Stalin died, the Jews' position improved slightly. But in the late 1950s, anti-Semitic and anti-Zionist attacks began again.

This new wave of anti-Semitism

JEWISH POPULATION IN THE EASTERN BLOC

Year	Soviet Union	Bulgaria	East Germany	Hungary	Yugoslavia	Poland	Czecho-slovakia	Rumania
1939	3,000,000	49,000	—	725,000	75,000	3,500,000	360,000	757,000
1984	1,630,000	35,400	900	63,000	5,100	4,800	8,700	30,000

The dais of the synagogue in the city of Tarnow, Galicia. It was destroyed during the Holocaust.

Far right: Shlomo Mikhoels (seated) in the role of King Lear, with a group of actors from the Jewish Theater in Moscow, 1935.

had one unexpected result: a number of Soviet Jews began to have strong feelings of Jewish nationalism. Many began studying Hebrew and visiting the few existing synagogues, and thousands asked to move to Israel. The Soviet leaders reacted by punishing those who led the struggle to leave. However, beginning in the late 1960s, sympathetic people—and countries—in the western world put pressure on the Soviet Union and the government began to allow Jews to leave. Since 1970, 250,000 Jews have left the Soviet Union. Most of them came to Israel. The remainder immigrated to other countries, especially the United States. There are still several thousand Jews in the Soviet Union who have been refused permission to leave. These dissident Jews are known as "prisoners of Zion" or "Refuseniks."

The Jewish communities in the Soviet Union and other Eastern European countries are based mainly in the cities. In the larger cities, like Moscow, in which 265,000 Jews live, and Leningrad, where 165,000 live, Jewish life centers around the few remaining synagogues. However, anti-Semitism and the pressures of life in the cities are causing many of them to assimilate, to lose their Jewish identity.

Small numbers of Jews are scattered throughout the various republics of the Soviet Union. Unlike in the big cities, there have been practically no mixed marriages among the Jews of the Caucasus and Central Asia. In Bukhara, for example, there were once about 45,000 Jews. The remaining Jews continue to live according to tradition and within the family framework; the Jewish communities there have kept their special character.

There is no official body to organize Jewish religious and social activities. A newspaper and a magazine in the Yiddish language, and two amateur acting troupes—one in Birobidzhan and the other in Vilna—are the curators of Jewish culture in the Soviet Union.

The government's efforts to take the Jews' identity from them, the high rate of intermarriage between Jews and non-Jews, and the unfair treatment of Jews in places of work and education—all are endangering the future of the Jewish community in the U.S.S.R.

EASTERN EUROPE

In the first few years after World War II, Holocaust survivors in Eastern Europe were busy trying to get their own lives back to normal. Different organizations, including Zionist movements, began to be active again. Zionist emissaries started preparing the Jewish communities for immigration (aliyah). But at the same time, the Soviet Union was taking over these countries, and the Zionist ideals clashed with Communist interests. The governments of Hungary, Bulgaria, Poland, and Rumania did allow some Jews to emigrate during the 1950s, and most of them went to Israel.

Although there are not many Jews

The Leningrad synagogue, below left.

Below center: A synagogue in Tashkent, Bukhara, with characteristic tapestries.

The Soviets have often used anti-Semitic cartoons in their propaganda against Zionism and Israel. Most link the Zionist movement with Nazism. Jews are pictured as ugly and twisted: Jews as spiders, with long hooked noses, etc. The message below is clear: A Jewish-Zionist plot threatens world peace.

Bottom: A demonstration in Israel, in support of Soviet prisoners of Zion.

Right: The Dohany Synagogue in Budapest.

Far right: Magen David (the Star of David) over a synagogue entrance in Seged, Hungary, from the 19th century.

Rabbi Emanuel Rosen, shown at right with Rumanian Premier Nicolae Ceausescu, is a member of the Rumanian National Assembly.

left in the countries of Eastern Europe, anti-Semitism continues. Nevertheless, Jewish citizens are allowed to run their own social and cultural affairs. The Jews of Rumania enjoy much freedom to develop religious, cultural, and social activities. They have their own newspaper, and they are allowed to immigrate to Israel. In Budapest, the capital of Hungary, there is a seminary for rabbis, which is the only one of its kind in the Eastern Bloc. The Hungarian people are eager to come to grips with their own role in the Holocaust, and Jewish subjects often appear in Hungarian literature and movies.

The Hungarian government is also making efforts to repair and keep up Jewish historical sites. The Jews of Rumania, Hungary, Czechoslovakia, and Yugoslavia keep in touch with Jewish organizations in other countries and even receive outside aid.

Unless the dramatic changes in the policy of openness under Soviet premier Gorbachev take place, there is a real danger that the Jewish people will eventually disappear from this part of the world.

27

THE JEWISH PEOPLE TODAY

Before World War II, the world Jewish population grew to about 17 million. From 1750 to 1940, the Jewish population increased almost seventeen-fold. This growth took place mainly among the Jews of Eastern Europe. During World War II, six million Jews were murdered in Europe. After the Holocaust, the birth-rate dropped. In addition, the growing number of mixed marriages has caused the assimilation of hundreds of thousands of Jews.

In 1987, only a quarter of the Jewish people—about 3.7 million—lived in Israel. The largest Jewish population lives in the U.S.A.—about 5.7 million people. About 1.74 million Jews live in the Eastern Bloc countries.

The largest Jewish community in the west, apart from the U.S.A., lives in France—more than half a million people. Anti-Semitism, which has increased in the 1970s and 1980s, has not spared France. In the heart of Paris, the Rue Copernique Reform Synagogue was attacked in

the early 1980s, and a bomb was thrown at a Jewish restaurant in the city's Jewish quarter. These acts, together with the anti-Zionist and anti-Israel attitudes of the French government, have intensified the strong feeling of Jewish identity among many French Jews. Despite this, there is a high rate of assimilation, which is endangering the Jewish community of France.

About 400,000 Jews live in Great Britain. Many of the Jewish families have been living there for several generations. Although many British Jews intermarry and assimilate (about 20%), there is also a strong Jewish awareness. Britain has many Jewish schools and Jewish cultural activities.

Canada is another country where many Jews live. Most of Canada's 300,000 Jews arrived there during the last few decades.

The Jews of Argentina number about 200,000, many having gone there after the Holocaust. They set up social and Zionist organizations.

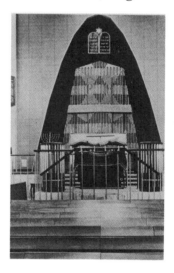

A synagogue in St. John's Wood, London, England.

The chart at far left shows the changes in the Jewish population since the beginning of the 19th century.

Left: A poster for a sports competition held in Buenos Aires, Argentina.

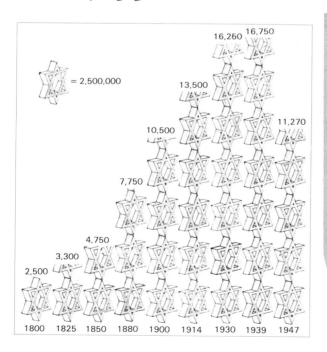

This Paris bakery displays a certificate issued by a local Jewish religious authority. It states that the food is prepared according to Jewish law.

Elderly Jews meet in the park in São Paolo, Brazil.

Far right: Jewish girls from Ethiopia in an Israeli school.

Planting trees in Capetown, South Africa, on Tu B'Shvat—the holiday celebrating the new year for trees.

populations of 5,000–7,000 each: Austria, Denmark, Greece, Colombia, and Peru. A few thousand Jews are left in Ethiopia, out of a community which numbered about 26,000 in 1984. Most came to Israel in 1985–1986 in a secret operation, following the terrible drought and famine which struck the area. Small pockets of Jewish communities can be found in Tunisia, India, Iran—where many left following the overthrow of the

About 120,000 Jews live in South Africa. Thousands of South African Jewish children attend Jewish schools and belong to Zionist youth movements.

In Brazil there is much Jewish cultural activity. More than 150,000 Jews in Brazil are organized within the framework of a Jewish federation. However, only one quarter of Brazil's Jewish youngsters receive any Jewish education.

Between 30,000 and 40,000 Jews live in each of the countries of West Germany, Italy, and Belgium. The Jewish communities of Mexico and Uruguay are of similar size, and enjoy widespread Jewish activity. About 26,000 Jews live in Holland and about 20,000 each in Switzerland, Chile, Venezuela, and Turkey. In Morocco there are about 15,000 Jews, who keep close ties with their brethren in Israel. Sweden, too, has about 15,000 Jews.

In Spain, from which the Jews were expelled 500 years ago, there now live about 12,000 Jews. The following countries have Jewish

Shah—Syria, Panama, and in several other countries.

The Jewish people are indeed scattered among other peoples, and this is one of the biggest problems of the community's existence.

JEWISH IDENTITY
In the Diaspora (all the countries of the world apart from Israel where Jews live—from the Greek word meaning "to scatter") the Jewish community has had to make an effort to keep its Jewish identity.

A Jewish identity is a mixture of religious, traditional, historical, and national components. A weakening of one of these components often weakens Jewish identity as a whole. Jews who become less religious and more secular lose some of their Jewish identity. The religiously observant Jew, for example, understands that which sets him apart from others in the non-Jewish society surrounding him. But the secular Jew is more affected by the culture in which he lives.

Some Jewish communities used to

116

be organized in such a way as to encourage the building of a Jewish identity. In America, and in other parts of the Diaspora today, most Jews live the kind of lives which leave no room for such identities. Language, for example, expresses a people's culture. Most of the Jews in the Diaspora no longer speak a separate language, such as Yiddish or Hebrew, and know only the language of the culture around them. Jewish leaders are becoming more and more aware that a Jewish education is important and necessary to develop a Jewish identity in the Diaspora. This can best be achieved in those communities which have a network of Jewish schools, and encourage religious and Zionist youth movements and summer camp activities.

Many Jews from the Diaspora visit Israel, and a study period in Israel is now part of the Jewish education of many students.

Jews have maintained a vibrant community outside Israel for more than 2,000 years. Despite the inroads of modern culture, they continue to flourish in the United States and other countries. And yet it is the rebirth of the Jewish state which unites Jews and gives them a renewed sense of belonging and pride in their Jewishness.

Far left: The Jewish holiday festival of Lag B'omer *(the 33rd day after Passover) is celebrated in the island of Djerba, off the Tunisian coast. According to legend, a plague among the pupils of Rabbi Akiva (2nd century* C.E.*) ended on this date. There are about 1,000 Jews living on the island today.*

An appeal to American students: a poster advertising the Israeli kibbutz.

28

JERUSALEM THROUGH THE AGES

The Western Wall is also known as the Wailing Wall. The photograph below is from the turn of the century.

Two mizrah *("East," to indicate directing one's prayers toward Jerusalem) papercuts from the late 19th century. The papercut at bottom right has a raised platform in its center which symbolizes the altar of the Holy Temple. Above it is a seven-branched lamp which is now the symbol of the State of Israel. Next to the altar are two pillars which stood in the Holy Temple. At the top are the Ten Commandments, and the deer in the middle are traditional Jewish symbols. The papercut at right is decorated with different animals and birds. The lions in the center are symbols of Jerusalem.*

Jerusalem is the only city in the world that is sacred to half the world's population—Jews, Christians and Muslims.

A HOLY CITY UNTO ISRAEL

Jerusalem became a holy city for the Jewish people around 960 B.C.E. when King Solomon, David's son, built a Temple so that the people could worship God in the capital of his kingdom. The Temple became the religious center for the Israelites.

In 586 B.C.E., Jerusalem, together with the First Temple, was destroyed and the Israelites were exiled. This only made the city more holy in their eyes. When they were permitted to return to their land in 538 B.C.E., they turned to Jerusalem first of all. They built the Second Temple, which stood for 600 years.

During this time, Jerusalem and the Temple remained the spiritual heart of the entire Jewish people. In Eretz Yisrael as well as in the Diaspora, they would turn to face the city in prayer, make pilgrimages, and send contributions.

During most of this time, the land was ruled by foreign conquerors—Persians, Greeks, Romans. However, when the Holy Temple was plundered during the reign of Antiochus IV Epiphanes, it sparked the Maccabean Revolt. Once more the Jews were independent. Their independence lasted about 80 years (141–63 B.C.E.), and ended when the Romans conquered the country. During the reign of King Herod (37–4 B.C.E.), Jerusalem was built up and improved. At that time, there were about 100,000 people living in the city.

Yet it was the Romans who, in the end, burned the Temple and destroyed Jerusalem, during the Great Revolt of 70 C.E. The Western Wall of the Temple

Mount, on which the Holy Temple was built, survived the destruction and remains standing to this day. It became a sacred place, and throughout the ages—when Jews were permitted to enter Jerusalem—they have come here to mourn the Temple's destruction and to pray for Redemption and put notes with requests to God in the cracks in the wall.

In countries west of Jerusalem, it is customary for Jews to fix an ornament called the *mizrah*—"East"—on the eastern wall of their houses and synagogues. It points to Jerusalem and the Temple. Throughout the ages, worshipers in the Diaspora have faced this direction in prayer.

The memory of the Temple has been kept alive on coins, in mosaic floors of many synagogues, and in book illustrations. The destruction of the Temple is remembered on fast days and even at celebrations. To this day, a glass is traditionally broken by the bridegroom during the wedding ceremony in remembrance of the Temple's destruction.

CHRISTIAN AND MUSLIM LINKS

Jesus was active—and was later crucified and buried—in Jerusalem. This fact makes the city holy for Christians. When the city fell into the hands of the Byzantine Christians (324 C.E.), they built many churches. The Church of the Sepulcher was built on the very spot where, according to Christian tradition, Jesus was buried. Along the Via Dolorosa—which, according to Christian tradition, was the path along which Jesus was led to his crucifixion—churches and other Christian buildings have been built. After the city was conquered by Muslim Arabs in 638, the Christians continued to treat Jerusalem as a holy city.

The city became Christian once

again when the Crusaders conquered it in 1099. They killed all non-Christians in it and made it their capital. Many pilgrimages were made until 1187, when Muslim Arabs once more took over the city. It remained under Muslim rule until 1917.

Jerusalem is also holy to the Muslim peoples. They have built two great mosques in the city—The Dome of the Rock and the El-Aqsa Mosque. Both were built on the Temple Mount during the Muslims' first period of rule. The Dome of the Rock was built in 691. According to Muslim tradition, the rock upon which it is built is the center of the universe. They believe that, on this spot, human souls are to be judged at the End of Days and sent to either Heaven or Hell. Tradition has it that Mohammed—the founder of Islam—rose to heaven from the nearby El-Aqsa Mosque.

The Muslim ruler Saladin conquered Jerusalem from the Crusaders in 1187, but those who came after him neglected the city,

Pilgrims along the Via Dolorosa as it is today.

The Temple Mount in a Jewish marriage contract from Padua, 1735, below left.

Bottom left: Eretz Yisrael, with Jerusalem at its center, on a mosaic map discovered in 1884 on a 5th-century Byzantine church floor in Transjordan.

Arabs. It was decided that Jerusalem would be under U.N. control so that all the religions could continue to worship there. However, as a result of the 1948 Israeli War of Independence, Jerusalem was divided between Israel and Jordan. The eastern part of the city, including the Old City and the Western Wall, was now controlled by Jordan. The new western part of

A church, a mosque, and a synagogue, drawn by a Jewish girl, from the worldwide exhibition "Children of the World Paint Jerusalem," above. The exhibition was held in 1977, in honor of the 10th anniversary of the reunification of Jerusalem.

The Old City—as drawn by Anna Ticho in 1917, above right.

The Dome of the Rock, above center.

Jerusalem, the center of the universe, on a map from the Crusader period, above far right. The Crusaders erected crosses on the Dome of the Rock, which became the Lord's Temple, and on top of the El-Aqsa Mosque, which became the Temple of Solomon.

and its population dwindled. In 1516, the Turks took over Eretz Yisrael. Suleiman the Magnificent rebuilt the walls around the Old City and repaired the water-supply system. But the city was again neglected, and in the year 1800, there were only 9,000 inhabitants.

A Jewish City Again

Early in the 19th century, the European powers became interested in Eretz Yisrael and Jerusalem. They helped the Christians living in the city and built churches, monasteries, hospitals, and charitable institutions. The Jewish population of the city began to grow, and in 1860 the first Jewish neighborhoods were built outside the Old City.

On November 29, 1947, the United Nations voted to divide Palestine between the Jews and the

the city was made the capital of the State of Israel on December 15, 1949. In the Six-Day War in 1967, Israel captured East Jerusalem and the Old City from Jordan, and on June 28, 1967, the two parts of Jerusalem were reunited into one city under Israeli law. Since then, the Israeli government and the Municipality of Jerusalem have given equal services to all the residents of Jerusalem, regardless of religion or nationality.

Jerusalem is the largest city in Israel. It is made up of different parts: the western part has Jewish residents; in the eastern neighborhoods most of the residents are Arabs; and within the Old City, in separate quarters, live Jews, Armenians, Muslims, and Christians. It serves as the spiritual center for people of all faiths all over the world.

120

Time Line of Jewish and World History

	Eretz Yisrael	Egypt	Mesopotamia, Assyria, Persia, Syria	Greece, Rome	
2000 B.C.E.	Patriarchs in Canaan		Hammurabi King of Babylon (1728-1686)		2000
1500	Exodus from Egypt (till 1280) The Israelites conquer Canaan (1250) Period of the Judges (1200-1020)	Rule of the Hyksos (1720-1570) Thutmose III (1450) Israelites in Egypt (1280) Ramses II (1290-1224)		Mycenaean Culture in Greece (1600) Destruction of Minoan Crete (1450) Trojan War (1200)	1500
1000	Saul, David, Solomon (1020-928) The Kingdom divided (928) Israel (928-720), Judah (928-586) Conquest of Samaria, the capital of Israel (729); Exile to Assyria (720) Campaign of Sennacherib to Judah (701) Destruction of Jerusalem, the first Temple, and exile to Babylonia (586); Cyrus'		Kingdom of Assyria (1300-587)	Homer (850); Founding of Carthage (814) Expansion of Greece Founding of Rome (800-600) The final Olympiad in Greece (776)	1000
500	proclamation Return to Zion (538); Building the Second Temple (520-515) Conquest by Alexander the Great (332) Ptolemies rule (301)	Destruction of Thebes (663) Persian conquest (525) Babylonia (539) Conquest of Alexander the Great (332); Ptolemies rule (322-30)	Sennacherib (704-681) Babylonia conquers Assyria (616) Nebuchadnezzar (605-562) Cyrus King of Persia conquers Babylonia (539) Conquest of Alexander the Great (332); The Seleucids rule Syria (330-75)	Solon Rules in Greece (544); Beginning of Roman republic (510); Battle of Marathon (490); Age of Pericles (461-429); Peloponnesian War (431-404) Alexander inherits the throne of Greece (336-323) First Punic War (264-241); Second Punic War (218-202)	500
C.E. 0	Seleucids rule (198) Hasmonean revolt (168); the Hasmonean Kingdom (160-63) Pompey in Eretz Yisrael (63) Birth of Jesus Crucifixion of Jesus (33) Jerusalem and the Second Temple fall (70); Judea made a Roman province (73); Bar Kokhba revolt (135)	Antiochus IV invades Egypt (168) Cleopatra VII (69-30) Riots against Jews of Alexandria (38); Jews revolt against Trajan (115)	Persecution of Christians (64)	Destruction of Carthage (146) Julius Caesar (100-44) Augustus (31 B.C.E.-12 C.E.) Reign of the Roman Emperors (14-217)	0
200	Editing of the *Mishnah* (210) Eretz Yisrael under Byzantine rule (324) *Jerusalem Talmud* completed (390)	**Jews of the East and North Africa** Mar Ukba exilarch (210-240)	**Jews of Europe** Jews in Cologne (321) Christian Church formulates its policy toward the Jews (325)	**World History** Beginning of Sassanid dynasty in Persia (224) Christianity made state religion in Roman Empire (340)	200
400		Jews forbidden to observe the Sabbath in Babylonia (455) *Babylonian Talmud* completed (500) Beginning of era of *Geonim* (589)	Justinian interferes in Jewish worship (553)	Last Roman Emperor in West deposed (476)	400
600	Jerusalem conquered by Persians (614-618) and by Umayyad Muslims (638) Eretz Yisrael conquered by Abbasids (750)	Muhammad fights Jews of Arabian Peninsula (623-629) Beginning of Muslim Empire (750)	Letters of Pope Gregory I fix church attitude toward Jews of Europe (mid-6th century) Persecutions of Jews in Visigothic Spain (612, 633, 638)	Pope Gregory I (590-604) Beginning of Muslim Calendar (622) Beginning of Muslim conquests (632) Charlemagne (768-814)	600
800	Conquest of Ahmad Ibn Tulun (878); Reign of Muhammad Ibn Tughj (922-946)	Calendar dispute between Babylonia and Eretz Yisrael (921); Death of Saadiah Gaon (942)	Jewish Khazar Kingdom (8th-10th century)	Carolingian Empire divided (843) King of Poland adopts Christianity (966); Unification of China under Sung dynasty (979)	800
1000	Seljuks conquer (1070-1078); Jerusalem conquered by Crusaders (1099) and by Saladin (1187)	Jewish center in Kairouan (10th century) R. Hezekiah b. R. David *gaon* and exilarch in Babylonia (1038-1058) Travels of Benjamin of Tudela (1160-73)	Expulsion of Jews from Mainz (1012); Death of Rabbenu Gershom *Meor-ha-Golah* (1028); Freedom of movement for Jews of England (1100)	Emperor Henry IV submits to the Pope in Canossa (1077) First Crusade (1096); Second Crusade (1147)	1000
1200	*Aliyah* of 300 French and English rabbis (1211) Mameluke rule (1291-1516) First *aliyah* of Jews and *Anusim* from Spain and Portugal (End of 14th century)		Burning of *Talmud* in Paris (1242) Disputation of Barcelona (1263) Charter of Boleslav V, in Poland (1264) Imprisonment of Jews in London (1278) Black Death massacres (1348) Jews of Italy granted charter (1348) Expulsions and blood libels from different places (14th-15th century)	Fourth Crusade: Byzantium conquered by Franks (1204); Genghis Khan conquers Asia (1206); Magna Carta (1215); Kublai Khan founds Yuan Dynasty in China (1264); Civil War in Japan (1333) Beginning of Hundred Years' War between France and England (1337) Black Death (1348) Peasants revolt in England (1381, 1383)	1200
1400		Jews of Ottoman Empire granted preferential status in commerce and crafts (1453)	Expulsion of Jews from Castile and Aragon (1492); Mass forced conversion in Portugal (1496)	Constantinople falls to the Turks; End of Hundred Years' War (1453) Vasco da Gama reaches India (1498)	1400
1500	Conquest of Eretz Yisrael by Ottoman Turks (1516) Ordination renewed in Safed (1538) Don Joseph Nasi leases Tiberias (1561)	Venice ghetto (1516) Burning of the *Talmud* in Rome (1533) Beginning of Jewish autonomy in Poland; Council of the Four Lands founded (1581) *Anusim* settle in Holland (1590)	Luther's 95 theses; Reformation (1517) Ivan the Terrible (1533-1584); Anglican Church founded (1534) Council of Trent; Counter-reformation (1545-1563) Peace of Augsburg (1555) St. Bartholomew's Day massacre (1572) Spanish Armada defeated (1588) Edict of Nantes (1598)	**American History** Development of American Indian civilizations (1200-1599) Columbus reaches America (1492) St. Augustine (Florida) founded (1565)	1500
1600	Center of Kabbalism in Jerusalem (1630-1660)	Chmielnicki massacres (1648-49) Massacre of Jews of Poland (1655-6) Jews of England granted religious freedom (1685)	Tokugawa shogunate rules Japan (1609) Dutch independence (1609) Louis XIII in France (1613-1643) Beginning of Thirty Years' War (1618) Charles I in England (1625-1649) Chmielnicki rebellion in Poland (1648-49) Ch'ing dynasty in China (1644) Louis XIV in France (1643-1715) Cromwell in England (1649-1660)	Jamestown founded (1607) Arrival of *Mayflower* (1620)	1600
1700	Judah Hasid and his group arrive in Eretz Yisrael (1700); Destruction of the *Ashkenazi* community of Jerusalem (1720); Renewal of Jewish community in Tiberias (1740); Hayyim Attar arrives in Jerusalem (1741); *Aliyah* of *Hasidim* (1746) Gedaliah Hayyun immigrates to Jerusalem; *Hasidim* arrive from Poland and Russia (1774)	The *Ba'al Shem Tov* and the beginning of *Hasidism* (1700-1760) Moses Mendelssohn (1729-1786) Jews in France given official recognition (1723); Legislation against Jews of Prussia (1750); Jews permitted to serve on city councils in Russia (1783); Full civil rights granted all Jews of France (1791); Pale of Settlement established (1791); Equal rights granted Jews of America (1792)	Portuguese reconquer Brazil (1654) The Glorious Revolution (1688-9) Peter the Great in Russia (1689-1725) War of the Spanish Succession (1701-14) England and Scotland united (1707) Beginning Hanover rule in England (1714) Seven Years' War (1756-1763) Louis XVI in France (1774-1792) French Revolution (1789) French Republic declared (1792) Napoleon becomes First Consul (1799)	Boston Tea Party (1773) Declaration of Independence (1776) Constitutional Convention (1787) Washington inaugurated (1789) Adams inaugurated (1797)	1700
1800	Napoleon in Eretz Yisrael (1799)				1800

Year	Eretz Yisrael, Zionism, Israel	Jews of the World	World History	American History
1800	First *olim* from Kurdistan (1812) Thirty Persian Jewish families arrive to settle (1815) Eretz Yisrael in hands of Muhammad Ali (1831) Restoration of Turkish rule in Eretz Yisrael (1840) First Jewish quarter outside city walls of Jerusalem (1856) Ghetto of Rome abolished (1870) Pinsker's *Autoemancipation* (1882) First *Aliyah* (1882) National Jewish Congress (1885) *Hovevei Zion* Conference (1887) Immigration from Russia (1891) Herzl's *Der Judenstaat* (1896) 1st Zionist Congress in Basle (1897)	Emancipation of German Jews (1808); Jewish quarters established in Morocco (1812); Restoration of rights to Jews of France (1818); Reform congregation in Charleston, S.C. (1824); British Parliament deliberates Jewish emancipation (1833) Anti-Jewish legislation in Russia (1939); Citizenship given to Jews of Turkey (1839); *B'nai B'rith* founded (1843); Emancipation for Jews of Germany (1848) Jewish craftsmen permitted to live outside the Pale (1865); Austro-Hungarian Jews granted rights (1867); German Jews granted rights (1871); Pogroms in Russia (1881); Jewish Theological Seminary founded in N.Y. (1886); Dreyfus trial (1894); Zionist Federation of America founded (1897); Union of Orthodox Synagogues founded (1898)	Napoleon crowns himself Emperor (1804) Napoleon invades Russia (1818) Congress of Vienna (1814-1815) Napoleon exiled to St. Helena (1815) Greek War of Independence (1821) 11 independent countries in South America (1826) July Revolution in France (1830) Opium War between Great Britain and China (1839) Revolutions of 1848 in Europe (1848) Louis Napoleon Emperor of France (1852) Japan opens door to trade with U.S.A. (1854) Crimean War (1854-1856) Opening of the Suez Canal (1869) Unification of Germany; Third Republic in France (1871) Chinese-Japanese War (1894-95) Boxer Rebellion in China Boer War in South Africa	Jefferson inaugurated (1801) Madison inaugurated (1809) Battle of New Orleans (1815) Monroe Doctrine (1823) Indian Removal Act (1830) The Battle of the Alamo (1836) War With Mexico (1846) Kansas-Nebraska Act (1854) Dred Scott Decision (1857) Lincoln elected (1860) American Civil War (1861-1865) Gold discovered in S. Dakota (1874) Electric light bulb invented (1879) Pindleton Civil Service Act (1883) Dawes Act (1887) Sherman Anti-Trust Act (1890); McKinley inaugurated (1897) Spanish American War (1898)
1900	4th Zionist Congress in London Herzl meets with Turkish Sultan Herzl *Altneuland* Uganda project Second *Aliyah*; Death of Herzl	Zionist groups in Syria and Morocco	Beginning of Bolshevism in Russia Russo-Japanese War	Theodore Roosevelt takes office Panama Canal Zone established
1905	7th Zionist Congress in Basle 8th Zionist Congress in The Hague	Pogroms in Russia; emigration to U.S.A. Dreyfus exonerated	Abortive revolution in Russia	Pure Food and Drug Act
1910	*Ha-Shomer* founded 10th Zionist Congress in Basle	Polish boycott against Jews H.I.A.S. founded in U.S.A. Beilis trial	Young Turk revolution Japan annexes Korea Sun Yat-sen President of China	Taft inaugurated
1915	*Hadassah* founded 13th Zionist Congress in Basle *Nili* spy ring established	*Alliance* school founded in Morocco American Joint founded	France conquers Morocco Balkan Wars World War I begins Sinking of the Lusitania Battles of Verdun; Sykes-Picot Agreement	Wilson inaugurated
1920	British conquer; Balfour Declaration Third *Aliyah*; British Mandate *Haganah* and *Histadrut* founded Arab riots in Jaffa Churchill "White Paper" League of Nations confirms Mandate Fourth *Aliyah*	Z.O.A. established American Jewish Congress founded Pogroms in Poland and Ukraine *Wizo* founded Hebrew schools opened in Poland	October Revolution in Russia Treaty of Brest-Litovsk Treaty of Versailles Polish-Russian War; Treaty of Sevres New Economic Policy (N.E.P.) in Russia Partitioning of Ottoman Empire Hitler's "beer-hall putsch" Death of Lenin *Mein Kampf* published	Wilson's Fourteen Points U.S. enters World War I Palmer raids U.S. Immigration Act sets 3% quota Teapot Dome scandal investigated
1925	Schism in *Gedud ha-Avodah* Hebrew University opened Jewish Agency established	Immigration restriction in U.S.A. Jewish settlement in Birobidzhan	Chiang Kai-Shek conquers China	Great bull market Stock market crash
1930	Passfield "White Paper" Schism in *Haganah; Izl* founded Youth *Aliyah* founded Fifth *Aliyah*	Pogroms in Salonika Economic boycott against German Jews Massacre of Iraqi Jews	Manchuria occupied Egypt and Iraq become independent Hitler becomes Chancellor of Germany	The First New Deal
1935	Arab Revolt; Massacres of 1936 proposal for partition MacDonald White Paper; General strike	Nuremberg Laws World Jewish Congress established Anti-Jewish legislation in Europe *Kristallnacht*	Ethiopia invaded Spanish Civil War Japan attacks China Austria annexed to Germany Beginning of World War II	The Second New Deal
1940	*Lehi* established *Palmah* established General strike for the Jews of Europe Jewish Brigade organized	43,000 refugees from Germany to U.S. Ghettos in Poland "Final Solution" drafted; Mass deportations to death camps; Uprising in the ghettos Extermination of Hungarian Jewry	Germany conquers other countries in Europe Germany invades U.S.S.R. Allies invade North Africa Battle of Stalingrad D-Day; Allied victories in Pacific Germany surrenders; atom bombs	U.S. enters World War II Roosevelt elected to 4th term
1945	Anglo-American committee for Palestine Illegal immigrants deported to Cyprus UN resolution for partition; War of	Holocaust total 6 million Pogroms against Jews of Poland Massacres of Jews in Iraq and Persia	Eastern Bloc established Paris Peace Conference; Marshall Plan	
1948	Independence; State of Israel founded; Ben-Gurion P.M., Weizmann President	Suppression of Jewish culture in U.S.S.R. Yemenite Jews move to Israel	Berlin blockade; Gandhi assassinated China—Republic; N.A.T.O. estab. 1948	Truman Doctrine
1950	Mass *aliyah* Border tension *Knesset* deliberates German reparations Attacks by Arab infiltrators Mass immigration from Morocco	Jews of Iraq move to Israel Prominent Jews executed in U.S.S.R. "Doctors' plot" in U.S.S.R. Jewish lobby in Washington organized Nahum Goldmann President of W.Z.O. Jews expelled from Egypt	Korean War End of state of belligerency between Germany and West Korean Armistice; Death of Stalin French defeated in Indochina Signing of Warsaw Pact	Eisenhower inaugurated McCarthy investigations
1955	Yarkon-Negev water pipeline opened Sinai Campaign Withdrawal from Sinai Hostilities along Syrian border		Revolts in Hung. and Poland; Suez crisis Vietnamese Civil War; 1st Soviet satellite Civil War in Lebanon Cuban Revolution	Eisenhower elected to 2nd term Federal troops sent to Little Rock U.S. troops sent to Lebanon Khrushchev-Eisenhower summit in U.S.
1960	Eichmann brought to Israel Ben-Gurion resigns; Eichmann trial I.D.F. operation in Syria Levi Eshkol prime minister National Water Carrier completed	Wave of anti-Semitism in Europe Pogroms in Jewish areas of Algeria Soviet Jews imprisoned Jewish self-defense in New York	Sino-Soviet conflict First man in space—Yuri Gagarin War between India and China Coup in Iraq Cairo Conference of Non-Aligned States	Kennedy elected U.S. president Bay of Pigs invasion Cuban missile crisis John Kennedy assassinated
1965	Relations with W. Germany Recession in Israel Six-Day War El-Al airliner hijacked to Algeria War of Attrition; Golda Meir P.M.	Vatican Council denounces anti-Semitism Wave of anti-Semitism in Poland Jews executed in Iraq	War between India and Pakistan Show trial of writers in U.S.S.R. Civil War in Nigeria Soviet invasion of Czechoslovakia Qaddafi ruler in Libya Sadat president of Egypt	American offensive in Vietnam Rise of "Black Power" Martin Luther King assassinated Neil Armstrong lands on the moon
1970	Massacre of children at Avivim Massacre of Israeli athletes in Munich Yom Kippur War; Death of Ben-Gurion Disengagement Agreements with Egypt	Leningrad trials U.S. Reform Movement moves center to Jerusalem 50 *aliyah* activists arrested in Soviet Union	China joins U.N.; Helsinki S.A.L.T. talks Vietnam ceasefire Death of Juan Peron in Argentina Civil War in Lebanon	Beginning of detente Watergate break-in Nixon resigns
1975	Palestinian terrorist actions Operation Jonathan in Entebbe Sadat visits Jerusalem Camp David talks; Operation Litani Carter visit; Camp David Accords signed	U.N. censures Zionism First congress on Yiddish in Jerusalem Demonstration in N.Y. for Soviet Jewry Trial of Anatoly Sharansky in U.S.S.R. One thousand Jews flown out of Iran	Race riots in South Africa Dang Xiaoping ruler of China Military coup in Afghanistan Islamic revolution in Iran	Jimmy Carter inaugurated
1980	Palestinian terrorist action Iraqi atomic reactor bombed Beginning of Lebanon War Begin resigns, Yitzhak Shamir P.M. National Unity Govt.; S. Peres P.M.	Bombing of synagogue in Paris Attacks on Jewish sites in Vienna Antwerp and Rome Hundreds of Jews arrested in Iran Most Ethiopian Jews brought to Israel	Civil War in El-Salvador; Iraq-Iran War "Solidarity" in Poland; Sadat assassinated Falklands War Fight against P.L.O. rebels Indira Gandhi assassinated	U.S. hostages taken in Iran U.S. grain boycott of U.S.S.R. Reagan inaugurated; *Columbia* shuttle American hostages freed from Iran Reagan reelected
1985	I.D.F. withdrawal from Lebanon Diplomatic relations with Spain	Waldheim blamed for hiding Nazi past	Escalation in Iran-Iraq War Corazon Aquino president of Philippines Openness (*Glasnost*) policy of U.S.S.R.	Reagan-Gorbachev summit *Challenger* space-shuttle disaster
1987	Ivan Demajanjuk trial			

GLOSSARY

The terms which appear in this glossary are used in the Encyclopedia. Most of them are Hebrew and refer to concepts in Judaism and Zionism. When two words, separated by a comma, appear together as the headword, the second is the plural form. A phonetic pronunciation appears in parentheses.

aliyah (ah-lee-yáh)
Hebrew for "going up." The word used for the immigration of Jews to Israel.

amora, amoraim (ah-mó-rah, ah-mo-rah-éem)
From the Aramaic word *amora*, which means "spokesman" or "interpreter." It refers to the sages from the time of the completion of the Mishnah (in the 3rd century), to the completion of the Talmud (in the 6th century). They interpreted the sayings of earlier sages and resolved the differences between the Mishnah and other writings.

anusim (ah-noo-séem)
Hebrew for "forced ones." Jews who were forced to convert to Christianity.

bar
Aramaic for "son of."

Bilu (bée-lew)
The first letters of the Hebrew words for the Biblical verse: "House of Jacob, come ye and let us go" (Isaiah 2:5). A Zionist organization in Russia founded in the late 19th century that supported immigration to and settlement in Eretz Yisrael.

diaspora (die-ás-pur-uh)
Area of Jewish settlement outside Eretz Yisrael.

gaon, geonim (gah-ohń)
A title for the heads of the Jewish Academies (*yeshivot*), most notably in Babylonia between the 6th and 11th centuries. The Hebrew word *gaon* means "a very wise man."

ghetto (gét-toe)
A special quarter for Jews in some European towns dating from the 16th century. Before World War II, Jews often chose to live in ghettos where it was easier to preserve a Jewish way of life. During World War II, they were forced into ghettos and from there were taken to death camps.

Habad (kha-báhd)
The first letters of the Hebrew words for "wisdom, understanding, knowledge." A branch of Hasidism. It began in Byelorussia, in a town called Lubavitch, and therefore these Hasidim are called Lubavitchers and their rabbi, the Lubavitcher Rebbe.

Hadassah (ha-dás-uh)
The federation of Zionist women in America. Its activities in Eretz Yisrael began with health and medical care, and then grew to include social and educational projects.

Haganah (ha-ga-náh)
Hebrew for "defense." The

The *Haganah* members trained for close combat with sticks instead of rifles.

defense force of the Jewish community in Palestine. The Haganah laid the foundations for the Israel Defense Forces (I.D.F.).

Haggadah (ha-ga-dáh)
Hebrew for "telling" or "tale." A collection of blessings, prayers, commentaries, and hymns read at the Seder, the Passover feast.

This illumination from the Sarajevo *Haggadah* of the 14th century shows Jacob's Ladder.

Halakhah (ha-la-kháh)
Hebrew for "walking"—a reference to walking in the path of righteousness. The part of the Talmud which contains laws and regulations set down by the ancient rabbis, after centuries of discussion, to interpret the Biblical commandments.

Hanukkah (kha-noo-káh)
Hebrew for "dedication." An eight-day holiday celebrated from the 25th of Kislev (the Jewish month which usually falls in December) in honor of the rededication of the Temple in Jerusalem after it was purified by Judah Maccabee.

Ha-Shomer (ha-show-méhr)
Hebrew for "the Guard." An organization of Jewish patriots in Eretz Yisrael founded in 1909 to preserve life, dignity, and property.

Hasid, Hasidism (kha-seéd, kha-seéd-ism)
The word *hasid* literally means a God-fearing person who observes the commandments. Today the word *hasidim* refers to the followers of the movement called Hasidism. The movement stresses the importance of devoutness in prayer, of serving God with joy while leading a normal, everyday life, and of absolute faith in the rabbi at the head of the community.

heder (kháy-der)
Hebrew for "room." A religious school for young Jewish children.

He-Halutz (heh-kha-loótz)
The World Federation of Zionist Youth—"the Pioneer" in Hebrew—founded in Russia in 1917. Its principles were based upon personal fulfillment by immigrating to Eretz Yisrael and settling there. The members were called *Halutzim* or pioneers.

Histadrut (hiss-tah-drút)
The General Federation of Labor in Israel, founded in 1920. A trade union whose members include most of the salaried and self-employed workers.

Hovevei Zion, Hibat Zion (kho-vuh-váy tsee-yón, kʼhee-baht tsee-yón)
Hebrew for "lovers of Zion" and "love of Zion." An organization

On May Day, the international workers' holiday, the *Histadrut* shows its solidarity with workers all over the world.

that began in Russia after the pogrom in 1881. Its members believed that Jews could live securely only in Zion (the Biblical name for Eretz Yisrael).

ibn (iʰb-un)
Arabic for "son of."

I.Z.L. (éts-el)
The initials of the Hebrew name of the National Military Organization, a Jewish underground organization active during the British Mandate.

Jewish Agency
The executive branch of the World Zionist Organization. During the British Mandate, the Jewish Agency was recognized as the representative of the Jewish people on all matters concerning the establishment of the Jewish national home in Palestine. Today, the Jewish Agency and the World Zionist Organization are the same thing. Their major activities now include aiding Jews in immigrating to Israel, immigrant absorption in the country, and settlement.

Kabbalah (kah-bah-láh)
The theory of Jewish mysticism and hidden wisdom. The word *Kabbalah* means "acceptance" in Hebrew. Kabbalistic theory is based on the desire for man's soul to rise and rejoin the Divine source from which it came. In order to do this, the individual must not only observe the Commandments, he must also pray and study the Torah with a special devotion achieved through fasting, self-inflicted suffering, and a study of the hidden meanings of the Hebrew words and letters.

kehillah, kehillot (keh-hee-láh, keh-hee-lóht)
Hebrew for "community," from the word *kahal*—a group of people. The organizational framework in which Jews throughout the world have lived.

kibbutz, kibbutzim (kee-boóts, kee-boót-seém)
Hebrew for "group," "grouping," "gathering together." A form of

settlement which exists only in Israel. Its members believe in communal living and equality in all aspects of production, consumption, and education.

Knesset (kuh-néss-et)
The parliament of Israel.

Lehi (léh-khee)
The first letters of the Hebrew name of the Fighters for Freedom of Israel, an underground organization active during the British Mandate.

Mandate
The period during which the British governed Palestine (1920–1948). Great Britain was given a mandate, or authority, by the League of Nations to administer the country.

mellah (meh-lah)
The term for a Jewish quarter in North African towns.

The official seal of the State of Israel includes the *Menorah* and olive branches.

menorah (meh-no-ráh)
Hebrew for "lamp." A ritual object of the Temple, it is a seven-branched candelabrum of gold, decorated with cups, knobs, and flowers. The menorah has become a symbol of the Jewish people and appears on the official seal of the State of Israel.

Mishnah (mish-náh)
From the Hebrew for "study" or "repetition." The system of Jewish law which developed and evolved until it was organized by Yehudah Ha-Nasi at the beginning of the 3rd century.

A *Nahal* soldier working as a shepherd.

Nahal (náh-khal)
The first letters of the Hebrew name of the Fighting and Pioneering Youth, a corps in the I.D.F. which combines military training with agricultural settlement. Nahal soldiers establish settlements in border areas and unpopulated regions of the country.

Nili (née-lee)
The first letters of the Hebrew words for The Eternal One of Israel Will Not Lie, a Jewish espionage organization in Eretz Yisrael during World War I. Its members aided the British Army in the hope that the British would take control of the country and allow the Jews to establish a national home in Eretz Yisrael.

olim (oh-leém)
Hebrew for "people who go up." A term for immigrants to Israel.

Palmach (pahl-mákh)
The first letters of the Hebrew words for "assault companies," the fighting corps of the Haganah which operated from 1941 through Israel's War of Independence.

Pesah (péh-sakh)—Passover
A holiday celebrated on the 15th day of Nisan (the Jewish month which falls around April or May) and lasting for seven days in Israel and eight days in the Disapora. (The English name of the holiday is a translation from Hebrew.) It commemorates the Exodus from Egypt.

The *Seder* ceremony, on the first night of *Pesah,* is shown in this illumination from a German *Haggadah* of the 15th century.

Rabban, Rabbi (rah-báhn, ráb-eye)
From the Hebrew word *rav* which means "great." Titles given to the great sages and religious leaders.

Sanhedrin (sahn-heh-dreén)
From the Greek for "council of elders." The highest religious, judicial, and legislative institution of the Second Temple period.

Shabbat (shah-báht)—Sabbath
The seventh day of the week, from the Hebrew "to rest," because "God rested on the seventh day from all his work which He had done" (Genesis 2:2). All work of any kind is therefore forbidden on the Jewish Sabbath.

Talmud (tahl-moód)
A body of teaching, containing commentary and discussion of religious scholars on the Mishnah, produced over several centuries. The Talmud contains religious laws and rulings in the fields of law, medicine, health and agriculture, as well as the beliefs and philosophy of Judaism.

tanna, tannaim (tah-náh, tah-nah-eém)
From the Aramaic for "to study." The term used for the sages of the 1st to the 3rd centuries C.E. who took part in the creation of the Mishnah.

Torah (toe-ráh)—Pentateuch
The first of the three sections of the Bible, comprising five books: Genesis, Exodus, Leviticus, Numbers, and Deuteronomy. According to Jewish tradition, the Torah (the Book of the Covenant) was given in writing to Moses on Mount Sinai.

White Paper
Official report of government commissions in Britain and British colonies. Six White Papers were issued in Palestine between 1922 and 1939. The last of these recommended limiting the sale of land to the Jews and restricting Jewish immigration to Palestine.

yeshivah, yeshivot (yuh-shee-váh, yuh-shee-vóte)
Traditional Jewish academies for advanced study in Torah, Mishnah, and Talmud. Yeshivot have operated since the time of the Talmud.

Yom Kippur (yome kee-poór)
The Day of Atonement. A religious holiday from the Bible observed on the 10th day of Tishrei (the Jewish month which falls in September or October). On this day, man is judged by God, and so it is a day of repentance, fasting, and prayer for forgiveness.

zaddik, zaddikim (tsah-deék, tsah-dee-keém)
Hebrew for a "righteous person," a person outstanding in his faith and goodness. In Hasidism, the title *zaddik* refers to the rabbi at the head of the Hasidic community. He is considered to be a mediator between man and God and is therefore treated as the supreme authority on earth by his followers.

Zohar (zó-har)
Hebrew for "brightness." The central book of the Kabbalah, which consists of a mystical commentary on the Torah. It is said to have been written by Rabbi Simeon bar Yohai, but many scholars believe that its author was Moses de Leon who lived in Spain in the 13th century.

INDEX

ACKNOWLEDGMENTS

The numbers following each source refer to the page and the number of the picture on it. For example, 12-1 refers to the picture on page 12. The pictures on each page are numbered from left to right and from top to bottom.

The editors and the publishers wish to thank the following for their kind permission to reproduce illustrative material:

Israel Museum, Jerusalem: Jacket (clockwise from top)-5, 7, 10, 12, 13; 1; 2; 6-1, 2; 12-1, 13-2; 15-3; 18-2a, b, d; 19-1, 2; 22-1, 3, 4 (Jacket-1); 28-1; 29-1, 3; 35-2; 36-1; 37-3; 49-1; 50-1, 3, 4; 51-1 (Jacket-9), 2, 3; 54-3; 55-2, 3; 59-3, 4; 63-3; 67-2, 3; 68-1, 2, 3; 101-2; 114-2; 118-2; 119-2; 120-1, 2; 124-1, 125-2. **Israel Department of Antiquities and Museums,** Jerusalem: 5-1; 9-1, 2, 3; 10-2, 3; 14-2; 16-4; 18-3; 19-3; 20-1. **Beth Hatefutsoth: The Museum of the Jewish Diaspora,** Tel Aviv: 36-2; 38-2; 39-1, 2; 40-3; 41-3; 44-2, 3; 47-3; 51-5; 53-2; 57-1; 58-2, 4; 63-2; 74-1; 112-2 (photo: Paula Ruth Van Gelder, U.S.A.); 112-2; 113-2, 3; 114-1, 3; 116-2, 3, 4 (Jacket-4); 117-1; by courtesy of Mary Black, N.Y., from the exhibition "Beyond the Golden Gate": *Hadassah* N.Y.—108-3; New York Historical Society—73-3; Museum City of N.Y.—74-3; Jewish Museum—107-2. **Ghetto Fighters House in Memory of Yizhak Katznelson,** Kibbutz Lohamei Haghetaot: 82-3; 83-2, 4; 84-2, 3, 4; 85-1, 2, 3; 89-4; 90-3; 91-3. **Islam Museum,** Jerusalem: 35-1. **Mishkan le-Omanut,** Ein Harod: 118-1. **Reuven Rubin House,** Tel Aviv: 69-3. **Tel Aviv Museum:** 41-4; 62-1; 108-5 **American Jewish Historical Society,** Massachusetts: 72-3; **Central Zionist Archives,** Jerusalem: 51-4; 64-1, 2, 3, 4, 5; 65-3; 67-5; 68-2, 4; 69-1; 71-2; 75-1, 2; 76-1; 78-2; 79-3; 90-2; 109-1, 3; 123-1. **Central Archives for the History of the Jewish People,** Jerusalem: 62-2; 107-1; 112-3. **Haganah Archives,** Tel Aviv: 89-2; 90-1; 91-2; 93-2; 123-3. **Hamaccabi World Union Archives,** Kefar Hamaccabia: 115-3. **I.Z.L. Archives,** Tel Aviv: 89-1. **I.D.F. Archives,** Givatayim: 93-1; 96-1; 100-3. **The Jewish National and University Library,** Jerusalem: 33-3; 52-3; 57-3; 61-1; 66-2, 3; 68-3. **Jewish National Fund Archives,** Jerusalem: 71-4; 108-1. **Keren Hayesod Archives (U.J.A.),** Jerusalem: 52-4. **Institute for Labor Research in Memory of Pinhas Lavon,** Tel Aviv: 69-2; 76-2. **Yad Vashem Archives,** Jerusalem: 80-1; 82-1, 2; 84-1; 86-1, 2, 3; 87-1 **Granot, Central Agriculture Cooperative Society:** 102-4. **Hebrew**

Union College: 73-1; 110-1. **Hebrew University,** Jerusalem, Institute of Archeology: 15-1. **Holyland Hotel,** Jerusalem: 46-1. **Kibbutz Yad Mordechai:** 86-4 (Jacket-3). **Keter Publishing House,** Jerusalem: 110-3; 115-1. **Tel Aviv University,** Archeology Department: 16-1. **Yad Izhak Ben Zvi Institute,** Jerusalem: 67-1 **The British Museum,** London: 15-2 (photo: A. Hay); 16-2 (photo: A. Hay); 17-2; 18-2c. **The Brooklyn Museum,** N.Y.: 19-5. **Musée de Cluny,** Paris: 66-1. **Guggenheim Museum,** N.Y.: © Estate of Mark Rothko 111-3. **Kulturgeschichtliches Museum, Osnabrück:** 87-2. **Musée Nationale du Louvre,** Paris: 10-1. **Muzej Grada,** Sarajevo: 123-1. **New Jersey State Museum,** Trenton: 73-2. **Museo del Prado,** Madrid: 48-1. **Jewish Museum,** Prague: 41-1, 2. **Rijksmuseum,** Amsterdam: 17-1. **Semitic Museum,** Massachusetts: 39-3. **Statens Museum fur Kunst,** Kobenhavn: 57-2. **Yale University Art Gallery,** New Haven: 37-1 **Dargaud Editeur,** Paris: 116-1. Fuchs E., **Die Juden in der Karrikatur,** 1921: 80-1, 2; 81-1, 2. **Heinrich Heine Institut,** Düsseldorf, by courtesy of Harald Engel: 58-1. Peters J.P. & Thiersch H., **Painted Tombs in Necropolis of Marissa,** 1905: 21-2 (photo H. Raad); **Patrimonio Nacional,** Madrid: 40-1. **Penguin Books,** London: 81-3. **Society of Friends of Touro Synagogue,** Newport: 47-3. **Bodleian Library,** Oxford: 45-2. **Bibliotheque Nationale,** Paris: 4; 28-2; 34-2; 46-3; 53-1. **Biblioteca Apostolica Citta del Vaticano:** 41-5. **Bibliotheque Royale Albert Ier,** Bruxelles: 42-2; 43-1. **Hessische Landes- und Hochschulbibliothek,** Darmstadt: 42-3. **Library of Congress,** Washington: 54-1; 75-2. **National Library,** Leningrad: 32-2. **Sächsische Landesbibliothek,** Dresden: 40-2. **Staats-und Universitätsbibliothek,** Hamburg: 22-2. **Universitätsbibliothek,** Leipzig: 42-4. **Zentralbibliothek,** Zürich: 54-4 The publishers wish to thank the collectors who have so kindly allowed their work to appear in this book: **Max Berger,** Vienna: 61-2. **Yitzchak Einhorn,** Tel Aviv: 43-2; 44-1; 59-1 (5-3); 71-3. **Meir Gur-Aryeh** (Courtesy Yona Fischer), Jerusalem: 77-3. **Samuel Givon,** Tel Aviv: 79-2; **Isaac Meir Heschel,** the Zaddik of Medzibezh, Haifa: 6-3; **Franz Krausz,** Tel Aviv: 77-1 (courtesy D. Tartakover); 79-1 (courtesy A. Shamir). **Daniel Levinson,** Nahariya: 74-2. **Arie Navon,** Tel Aviv: 88-2; 95-2. **Gérard Silvain,** Paris: 56-1; 60-3; 62-4; 74-4. **Zionan Tadjar,** 77-2; 79-4. **D.**

Tartakover: 103-4; 124-2 (Shamir Brothers); 108-2 (Paul Kor)

Photographers
Bar-David Photo Agency: 111-1, 4. **Werner Braun,** Jerusalem: 14-3; 25-1 26-1; 27-1; 28-3 (Jacket-2); 29-2; 30-1, 2, 3, 4; 31-2, 3; 33-1, 2, 4; 54-2. **Theodore Cohen,** N.Y.: 109-2; 110-2. **Government Press Office,** Jerusalem: 89-3; 91-1; 92-3; 94-1, 4; 95-3; 96-3, 4; 97-2; 98-3, 4; 99-3, 4; 100-2; 103-1, 2; 104-1, 2, 3; 105-1, 2, 4; 106-1, 3, 5; 113-4. **Alex Gal,** Tel Aviv: 125-1; **Arie Ginton,** Kibbutz Maoz Hayim: 102-3. **Devorah Gruda,** Tel Aviv: 102-1, 2. **Abraham Hay:** 11-1, 2; 16-2; 32-1; 78-1; 94-3; 101-3; 106-2, 4. **Eyal Itzhar,** Jerusalem: 96-2; 99-1; 120-3. **David Katzir,** Kibbutz Dafna: 98-1. **Garo Nalbandian,** Jerusalem: 20-2; 25-2; 34-1. **Palphot:** 23-1; 105-3; Back Jacket. **Ze'ev Radovan,** Jerusalem: 67-4. **Riki Rosen,** N.Y.: 110-1, 4. **Ami Shamir,** Rehovot: 46-2; 47-1; 97-1, 3

Maps, Diagrams and Illustrations
Carta, Jerusalem: 11-3; 14-1; 18-1; 24-2; 43-3; 46-1; 47-4; 49-2; 52-1; 60-1; 87-3. **Dalia and Menahem Egozi:** 78-3, 4, 5; 92-2; 94-2; 98-2; 100-1; 103-3, 4. **Ehud Oren:** 12-2; 13-1; 16-3; 24-1; 31-1; 34-3; 38-1; 58-3; 60-4; 62-3; 65-2; 75-1, 4, 5; 76-3; 79-5; 83-2; 88-1; 95-1; 103-2; 115-3

Every effort has been made to locate the proprietors of copyrighted material used in this book. In the case of omissions, the Publisher will be pleased to make suitable acknowledgment in future editions.

Key to the front jacket illustrations: clockwise from top: the statue of Mordecai Anielewicz, the commander of the Jewish Fighters Organization in the Warsaw ghetto uprising, in Kibbutz Yad Mordechi, Israel; Jewish children plant trees on the holiday of *Tu B'Shvat* in Capetown, South Africa; a case for a Torah scroll from North Africa; Hebrew letters designed in Antwerp, Belgium, in the 16th century; a gold and enamel earring from Afghanistan; a Yemenite *tallit kattan,* worn always under the clothes by pious male Jews everywhere; a parade in honor of Israel's Independence Day in New York City, 1983; a coin from the Hasmonean Kingdom; a Jewish wine jug from 18th-century Syria; a Jewish marriage contract from 18th-century Italy; Masada, the last stronghold of the Jewish rebels after the Great Revolt in the year 70 C.E.; a Yemenite Jew in typical dress (center); Above: a clay oil lamp from the 1st century B.C.E.

On the back jacket: a view of Jerusalem with the Temple Mount in the center.